Martial

ANCIENTS IN ACTION

Catullus
Amanda Hurley

Cleopatra
Susan Walker and Sally-Ann Ashton

Horace
Philip D. Hills

Lucretius
John Godwin

Martial
Peter Howell

Ovid: Love Songs
Genevieve Liveley

Ovid: Myth and Metamorphosis
Sarah Annes Brown

Pindar
Anne Pippin Burnett

Sappho
Marguerite Johnson

Spartacus
Theresa Urbainczyk

Tacitus
Rhiannon Ash

ANCIENTS IN ACTION

MARTIAL

Peter Howell

BLOOMSBURY
LONDON • NEW DELHI • NEW YORK • SYDNEY

Bloomsbury Academic
An imprint of Bloomsbury Publishing Plc

50 Bedford Square
London
WC1B 3DP
UK

1385 Broadway
New York
NY 10018
USA

www.bloomsbury.com

Bloomsbury is a registered trade mark of Bloomsbury Publishing Plc

First published in 2009 by Bristol Classical Press

© Peter Howell 2009

Peter Howell has asserted his right under the Copyright, Designs and Patents Act, 1988, to be identified as Author of this work.

All rights reserved. No part of this publication may be reproduced or transmitted in any form or by any means, electronic or mechanical, including photocopying, recording, or any information storage or retrieval system, without prior permission in writing from the publishers.

No responsibility for loss caused to any individual or organization acting on or refraining from action as a result of the material in this publication can be accepted by Bloomsbury or the author.

British Library Cataloguing-in-Publication Data
A catalogue record for this book is available from the British Library.

ISBN: PB: 978-1-8539-9702-0
ePDF: 978-1-4725-2139-2
ePUB: 978-1-4725-2140-8

Library of Congress Cataloging-in-Publication Data
A catalog record for this book is available from the Library of Congress.

Contents

Preface	7
1. The Life of Martial	9
2. What is an Epigram?	35
3. Martial and the Epigram	49
4. Martial and Domitian	63
5. Martial and Roman Social Life	73
6. Martial and Patronage	93
7. Martial and Posterity	101
Further Reading	119
Index	123

Preface

When I was looking for a topic for my BPhil dissertation in 1963, and thought of Juvenal, my supervisor, Professor Robin Nisbet, suggested that I should choose Martial instead. I have remained sincerely grateful for the recommendation, as for his generous help and encouragement. At that time, hardly anything serious had been published on Martial (at any rate in English) for several decades. He was so little studied that no one seemed to have noticed that the chief difference between the first edition of W.M. Lindsay's Oxford Classical Text of 1903, and the second of 1929, was the omission of a page of 'Corrigenda et Addenda' – not incorporated into the text. The last forty years or so have seen a remarkable resurgence of interest in Martial, as the section on 'Further Reading' will show. The study of Juvenal, and of Roman social life, has also made great strides. This little book attempts to give an account of the man and his work, as seen from the early twenty-first century.

I am particularly grateful to the distinguished Martial commentators, and my loyal friends, Dr T.J. Leary and Dr Nigel Kay, whose criticisms and suggestions have been of incalculable assistance. Dr Edward Diestelkamp has helped with technical matters. The editor of the series, Deborah Blake, has shown sympathetic forbearance.

For Edward, after thirty years

1
The Life of Martial

Marcus Valerius Martialis – familiarly known in English as Martial – was born in about AD 40. We know this because he tells us in a poem published in about 95-98 that he was celebrating his 57th birthday (10.24). His third name (*cognomen*) came from his having been born on March 1st. We are better informed about his life than in the cases of most ancient authors because he tells us so much about himself, though care is needed as the first person singular may be the 'authorial' use, rather than personal.

He often writes about his birthplace Bilbilis, a small town in Hispania Tarraconensis. Its name must have been quite unknown, and rather odd-sounding, to almost all of his readers, even though Spain was by this time thoroughly Romanised. Martial's parents were called Fronto and Flaccilla (5.34). The names are Roman, but he makes it clear that he was a native Spaniard, with bristly hair and hirsute legs and cheeks (10.65).

Bilbilis stood on a rocky hill, above the steep winding valleys of the Rivers Jalón, on the east, and the Ribota, on the north. It was near the modern town of Calatayud in Aragon, between Zaragoza and Madrid. The surroundings were probably more wooded in ancient times, but are now mostly bare, apart from some vineyards and orchards. Martial mentions the local fruit, and you can still buy sweets called 'Frutas de Calatayud'. It was a remarkable site for a town, on the broad saddle between the two peaks of the hill, which falls precipitously on the north and east. The rocky crags are richly coloured. To the east and north the mountains are close, the highest being Moncayo (2,315 metres). To the south and west are wide plains, suitable for breeding the small, tough horses for which the region was famous. Its other chief product was iron, used to make weapons, which were tempered in the icy rivers. Martial also mentions the alluvial gold of the River Tagus (e.g. 1.49.15 – see below).

The site of the town has been excavated for some years, and there are remains of a bath-complex, numerous cisterns, and even a theatre. The most striking building must have been the temple, which stood on a projecting eminence, and formed a landmark for miles around.

Bilbilis had been given the status of a *municipium* in the time of Augustus. As a result, the magistrates and their families would have been Roman citizens. It appears that Martial was born a citizen, which suggests that his father may have been a magistrate. He tells us that he received the normal Roman education, in 'grammar' and oratory, widely available in Spain at this time.

In about 64 Martial moved to Rome. This was the obvious course for a talented provincial, and he was prob-

1. The Life of Martial

ably encouraged by the example of the other Spaniards who had made the same move, and contributed so much to Roman literary life in the first century AD. These included, from Cordoba, the two Senecas, father and son, authors respectively of rhetorical works, and of philosophy and tragedy, and Lucan, nephew of the younger Seneca, author of an epic poem on the civil war between Caesar and Pompey; Columella, from Cadiz, author of a treatise on agriculture; and Quintilian, from Calahorra, orator, teacher, tutor of Domitian's great-nephews, and author of a work on the education of the orator. The likelihood is that Martial too was envisaging a life in literature: he refers to youthful works in Book I (113). Literature, however, did not automatically bring in money, as there was no copyright law in the ancient world, and so no such thing as royalties. He must have been dependent on the patronage of rich benefactors, and there is reason to suppose that these included the younger Seneca and perhaps other members of the same family and circle.

However, in 65 a conspiracy was formed, the intention being to replace Nero with C. Calpurnius Piso. The suspected complicity of Seneca and Lucan led to their enforced suicides, as well as that of Piso. Piso had been known for his open-handed patronage (Martial refers to him, and the Seneca family, as generous patrons at 4.40, and so does Martial's near-contemporary, the satirist Juvenal), and in the aftermath it is likely that patrons were careful not to be so ostentatious in their generosity.

Modern writers sometimes take Juvenal at his own word when he implies that for a literary Roman there was no respectable source of income available other than patronage. The untruth of this is clearly revealed by Martial, who admits that the obvious source of income for a man like him was rhetoric, whether by teaching, or by pleading in the courts. Traditionally this latter had been regarded as a gentlemanly arrangement between friends, but under Claudius a law had finally made official the practice of 'rewarding' advocates. Martial represents Quintilian as advising him to take up advocacy, but replies that he prefers a quiet and enjoyable life. What he really meant was that the life of a poet could not be combined with that of a lawyer.

Admittedly at 3.38 he asks a fictitious Sextus, who is coming to Rome, how he intends to live there, since lawyers cannot even cover their rent, but this need not be taken seriously. He goes on to say that poets all freeze, and only three or four can live by cultivating great men. His answer to Sextus' dilemma is that, if he is a good man, he may live by luck. The implication is that if he is not 'a good man' he may do well, which reminds one of Juvenal's Umbricius (3.21f.), whose reason for leaving the city is that there is no place there for *honestae artes* (honourable pursuits); he goes on to describe in graphic detail how the unscrupulous prosper there.

Martial also gives a number of clues to show that such a life was not without pecuniary rewards. At 5.16 he jokingly claims that his readers owe him a debt:

1. The Life of Martial

Seria cum possim, quod delectantia malo
    scribere, tu causa es, lector amice, mihi,
qui legis et tota cantas mea carmina Roma:
    sed nescis quanti stet mihi talis amor.
nam si falciferi defendere templa Tonantis
    sollicitisque velim vendere verba reis,
plurimus Hispanas mittet mihi nauta metretas
    et fiet vario sordidus aere sinus.
at nunc conviva est comissatorque libellus
    et tantum gratis pagina nostra placet.
sed non et veteres contenti laude fuerunt,
    cum minimum vati munus Alexis erat.
'belle' inquis 'dixti: iuvat et laudabimus usque.'
    dissimulas? facies me, puto, causidicum.

As for the fact that, although I could write serious works, I prefer to write entertaining ones, you, friend reader, are my reason, you who read and recite my verses throughout the whole of Rome; but you do not know how much such affection costs me. For if I should wish to defend the temple of the sickle-bearing Thunderer [i.e. defend the interests of the Treasury], and to sell words to anxious defendants, very many sailors would send me Spanish oil-jars [barristers were often paid in kind, and olive oil was exported from Spain] and my pocket would become dirty with all sorts of coins. But as it is now my book is a dinner-guest and fellow-reveller, and my page pleases only when free of cost. But men of old were not equally content with praise, when the very least present for a bard was an Alexis. 'Nicely put', you say: 'it pleases us and we shall go on praising you'. Are you pretending not to understand? I think you'll make me a pleader.

'Alexis' (the name of a character in Virgil's second *Eclogue*, was believed (probably mistakenly) to have been a real slave-boy given to him by his wealthy admirer Asinius Pollio, though Martial several times refers to him as a gift from his better-known patron Maecenas, and twice (8.55; 73) claims that it was the love of Alexis which made Virgil a great poet, so that he too would welcome such a gift.

As an author, Martial concentrated entirely on the genre of epigram. This was a surprising choice. None of his Latin predecessors had restricted himself in this way (whether any Greek authors did so is unknown). He suggests a number of reasons for his decision. Some are not to be taken too seriously – for example, laziness, and a disinclination to undertake longer and more demanding genres. A negative one must have had more weight – his dislike for the mythological poetry, often in the form of epic, which was fashionable in Rome at that time. This vogue came about partly because Virgil had shown that the disapproval of longer forms of poetry expressed by the great Alexandrian poet Callimachus in the third century BC might not apply to a Roman poet, and that a great Latin epic could be

1. *The Life of Martial*

written, and partly (as Juvenal so memorably argued in his first Satire) because it was unlikely to give personal offence, and was politically harmless. The outstanding epic poet of Martial's time was Statius, who wrote a poem in twelve books on the story of the Seven against Thebes, and began another about Achilles. The fact that he never mentions Martial in his shorter poems, and that Martial never mentions him, has led to the supposition that they regarded each other with rivalry, if not hostility.

The avoidance of personal offence was a serious consideration. Lucan's 'modern' epic on the Pharsalian War, with its ecstatic praise of the great Republican hero, the younger Cato, was in effect a challenge, not just to Nero, but to the concept of autocracy. And Lucan had suffered for it.

Although we know that he had written poetry previously (as mentioned above), the earliest work of Martial to survive is the so-called *Liber Spectaculorum*, 'the book of the shows'. It has traditionally been held that it was written to celebrate the opening of the Flavian Amphitheatre (now known as the Colosseum) in 80, under the emperor Titus, but it has recently been convincingly argued by T.V. Buttrey that the book describes shows put on under his brother Domitian sometime between 83 and 85.

It may have been the writing of this book which won Martial the favour of Titus, who granted him the *ius trium liberorum* – the privileges of a father of three children – despite the fact that he had none. The privileges included the right to receive legacies. The *ius* was part of the

Augustan marriage legislation, intended to encourage people to have children. It is most unlikely that Martial was ever married. Although Domitian on his accession confirmed all the privileges granted by his brother, Martial published a poem asking for his to be renewed – presumably as an indication of imperial favour.

It is not known whether it was Titus or Domitian who gave Martial his titular tribunate. This sinecure army commission brought with it equestrian rank. The *equites* (knights) were in origin the cavalry, but by the imperial period the title simply denoted the rank below that of the senators. To hold it, a man had to possess at least 400,000 sesterces, an amount which would have produced enough income to enable a man to live respectably at Rome. It was not uncommon for men to be given money by rich friends so that they could meet the qualification. Martial himself refers to this, Pliny did it, and the conspirator Piso helped several men to acquire the rank every year.

After the *Liber Spectaculorum*, Martial produced two books, which are confusingly known nowadays as XIII and XIV. Both had Greek titles – *Xenia* (presents given to friends), and *Apophoreta* (presents to be taken away [from dinner parties]). Each contained a large number of two-line poems, like 'mottoes', describing or commenting on an immense variety of gifts.

It was only in about 86 that Martial brought out what he called his 'Book I'. This self-conscious decision was like that of a musical composer, who will not use the term

1. The Life of Martial

'Opus 1' until he feels that the work shows a proper maturity. It is, however, possible that Martial only designated this book 'I' when he published his 'Book II'. The first epigram is particularly striking:

> Hic est quem legis ille, quem requiris,
> toto notus in orbe Martialis
> argutis epigrammaton libellis:
> cui, lector studiose, quod dedisti
> viventi decus atque sentienti,
> rari post cineres habent poetae.

It's him! – the man whom you're reading is the man you're looking for, Martial, known throughout the whole world for his clever books of epigrams; to whom, enthusiastic reader, you have given a glory, while he is still alive and can appreciate it, which few poets have after their deaths.

Readers may feel surprised that an author, in the first poem of his 'first book', can make such a claim. Could he just be referring to the *Liber Spectaculorum*, the *Xenia*, and the *Apophoreta*, and also perhaps to the youthful works which he tells us at 1.113 have already been published? Would these have brought world-wide repute? It has been argued that Martial also wrote individual collections of a few poems each – *libelli*, or little books – for particular friends or patrons, or particular occasions, and that these had contributed to his fame. There is too the possibility that, if 'Book I' only received this title when Book II was published, this epigram was added then.

At the time of the publication of his first book, Martial lived in a flat up three flights of stairs, on the Quirinal Hill (1.117). The majority of the urban population of Rome lived in flats. He had a number of slaves, including two mentioned in Book I. One was a scribe, whose work had included copying poems to be sent to emperors (Titus and Domitian).

After the publication of Book I, Martial's books appeared with remarkable regularity, at intervals of one or two years, up to the publication of Book XI in 96. This was followed in 98, after the accession of Trajan, by the publication of a second edition of Book X, in which poems praising Domitian had presumably been replaced with others. The increase in his prosperity is shown by the fact that, sometime before 94, he acquired a small house, probably in the same part of Rome. He also owned a pair of mules, useful to get him to his small country estate at Nomentum (now Mentana), 15 miles north-east of Rome, which he had owned since at least about 83, and which produced wine and vegetables. It may have been given to him by the younger Seneca.

It was normal at Rome for richer men to give presents, often in the form of money, to their less well-off friends (see Chapter 6). Martial benefited from this, not least because he was in a position as a celebrated author to

1. The Life of Martial

reward their generosity by mentioning them in his poems. This was considered equally normal.

In one poem (5.20) Martial gives us a picture of how he would like to spend his days with his close friend Julius Martialis (the similarity of names does not indicate relationship):

Si tecum mihi, care Martialis,
securis liceat frui diebus,
si disponere tempus otiosum,
et verae pariter vacare vitae,
nec nos atria nec domos potentum
nec litis tetricas forumque triste
nossemus nec imagines superbas;
sed gestatio, fabulae, libelli,
campus, porticus, umbra, Virgo, thermae,
haec essent loca semper, hi labores.
nunc vivit necuter sibi, bonosque
soles effugere atque abire sentit,
qui nobis pereunt et imputantur.
quisquam, vivere cum sciat, moratur?

If I were permitted, dear Martialis, to spend days free from care with you, to arrange our time at leisure, and be free on an equal basis truly to live our lives, we should not be familiar with atria, or the homes of the more powerful citizens, or harsh law-suits and the wretched forum [where business was transacted], or proud busts [in the entrance-halls of the powerful], but driving, telling stories, light literature, the Campus Martius, porticoes, shade, the Aqua Virgo, hot baths, these would always be our haunts and the scenes of our labours. Now neither of us lives for his own benefit, and each is aware that the good days fly away and go off, are wasted by us and yet are reckoned up. Does anyone, who knows how to live, delay doing so?

Here Martial, like Juvenal, cites the need to call on 'more powerful citizens' as a bore, and the references to law-suits and the forum do not just indicate the risk of being involved in these oneself, but also the desire of these men to have a large entourage of supporters in such circumstances (more will be said about this later).

Martial's ideal life refers to literature in the words 'stories and light literature', but the hard work of writing was his chief occupation. We know from contemporary writers that authors regularly introduced their work by means of recitations. The younger Pliny (who reports that in one month of April there was a recitation on almost every day) regards attendance as a form of social obligation, and regrets that many people in his time would try to avoid accepting invitations: he, of course, is scrupulously assiduous.

Juvenal opens his first Satire by declaring that his chief aim in writing is to get his own back on other poets whose recitations he has been obliged to attend, and at the begin-

1. *The Life of Martial*

ning of his third Satire the list of the horrors of the city – fires, collapsing houses, and so on – culminates comically with poets who recite in August. Martial frequently refers to other authors' recitations, often as disagreeable, or even as opportunities for plagiarists to recite his works as their own, but rarely mentions himself doing it. Once he promises not to recite at his own dinner parties (11.52.16), while at 14.137 he suggests that a scarf is a useful present as it can block the ears when he recites. It would be a mistake to assume that he did in fact hardly ever recite his works. For one thing, it would have seemed churlish had he always refused when requested. And his works would have been much less tedious to hear than the epics and tragedies referred to by Juvenal. However, it is clear that Martial himself did not envisage this as the principal means by which his works would become known, since already at 1.1 he addresses his 'enthusiastic reader', and this is his usual practice.

The ideal life described by Martial at 5.20 is very much an urban one; but he later writes an epigram on the same subject, though a very different one (10.47):

Vitam quae faciant beatiorem,
iucundissime Martialis, haec sunt:
res non parta labore, sed relicta;
non ingratus ager, focus perennis;
lis numquam, toga rara, mens quieta;
vires ingenuae, salubre corpus;

prudens simplicitas, pares amici;
convictus facilis, sine arte mensa;
nox non ebria, sed soluta curis;
non tristis torus et tamen pudicus;
somnus qui faciat breves tenebras;
quod sis esse velis nihilque malis;
summum nec metuas diem nec optes.

The things which make life happier, most delightful Martialis, are these: wealth acquired not by labour, but by legacy; fruitful land, a permanently blazing hearth; never a law-suit, the toga rarely worn, a quiet mind; average strength, a healthy body; prudent straightforwardness, like-minded friends; easy companionship, dining without art; evenings not drunken, but free from anxieties; a bed not gloomy, but chaste; sleep which makes the darkness seem short; that you should wish to be what you are, and prefer nothing to it; that you should neither fear your last day, nor wish for it.

Here the setting is the countryside, and it is clear that Martial by this time had mixed feelings about the city. He had already, in about 87, sent Book III back from Forum Cornelii, the modern Imola, on the Via Aemilia between Bologna and Ravenna, though why he should have been staying in that surely very dull town is unknown. In his next book (4.25) he says that he hopes to retire to the

1. The Life of Martial

neighbourhood of Aquileia, at the north end of the Adriatic.

In a number of poems Martial had expressed his love for his homeland. His second longest poem, 1.49 (42 lines), eulogises it, by contrast with city life, the occasion being the return to Spain of his distinguished compatriot Licinianus:

Vir Celtiberis non tacende gentibus
    nostraeque laus Hispaniae,
videbis altam, Liciniane, Bilbilin,
    equis et armis nobilem,
senemque Caium nivibus, et fractis sacrum
    Vadaveronem montibus,
et delicati dulce Boterdi nemus,
    Pomona quod felix amat.
tepidi natabis lene Congedi vadum
    mollesque Nympharum lacus,
quibus remissum corpus astringes brevi
    Salone, qui ferrum gelat.
praestabit illic ipsa figendas prope
    Voberca prandenti feras.
aestus serenos aureo franges Tago
    obscurus umbris arborum;
avidam rigens Dercenna placabit sitim
    et Nutha, quae vincit nives.
at cum December canus et bruma impotens
    Aquilone rauci mugiet,

aprica repetes Tarraconis litora
    tuamque Laletaniam.
ibi illigatas mollibus dammas plagis
    mactabis et vernas apros
leporemque forti callidum rumpes equo –
    cervos relinques vilico.
vicina in ipsum silva descendet focum
    infante cinctum sordido;
vocabitur venator et veniet tibi
    conviva clamatus prope;
lunata nusquam pellis et nusquam toga
    olidaeque vestes murices;
procul horridus Liburnus et querulus cliens,
    imperia viduarum procul.
non rumpet altum pallidus somnum reus,
    sed mane totum dormies.
mereatur alius grande et insanum sophos:
    miserere tu felicium
veroque fruere non superbus gaudio,
    dum Sura laudatur tuus.
non impudenter vita quod relicum est petit,
    cum fama quod satis est habet.

O you who must always be remembered by the Celtiberian people, glory of our homeland Spain, you will see, Licinianus, lofty Bilbilis, renowned for horses and weapons, and old man Caius [Moncayo] with his snows, and sacred Vadavero with its jagged

1. The Life of Martial

mountains, and the sweet grove of delicious Boterdus, which fertile Pomona loves. You will swim in the smooth shallows of Congedus and the soothing lakes of the Nymphs, and when your body is relaxed by these you will brace it in the narrow Salo, which cools iron. There Voberca will provide you while you lunch with wild beasts which can be hit from close at hand. You will overcome the cloudless summer heat by the gold-bearing Tagus [Tajuña], sheltered by the shade of the trees; icy Dercenna and Nutha, which beats even snow, will satisfy your greedy thirst. But when hoary December and ruthless mid-winter bellow with hoarse Aquilo [the north-north-east wind], you will seek again the sunny shores of Tarraco [Tarragona] and your Laletania [Catalonia]. There you will slaughter hinds caught up in pliant nets and home-bred boars, and you will drive the hare to collapse on your stout horse, but the stags you will leave for your bailiff. The neighbouring wood will come down to the hearth itself, which is surrounded by dirty infants; your huntsman will be invited and will come along to be your guest, after you have shouted from close to. Nowhere is to be seen the crescent-decorated leather shoe [of a magistrate], nowhere the toga or clothes smelly with purple-fish. Far away are the shaggy Liburnian [a herald slave] and the querulous client, far away are imperious widows. The pale defendant will not interrupt your deep slumber; instead you will sleep all morning. Let someone else earn the loud 'Bravo!' [in the law-courts, or recitation hall]; you should pity the successful, and, free from pride, enjoy real happiness, while your friend Sura wins praise. There is no shame if a man seek to live to the full as much life as is left to him, when his reputation has achieved enough.

At last, in 98 or soon after, Martial decided to return home. His frequently expressed nostalgia might seem sufficient explanation for this, now that he was around sixty years old, but some have thought that a contributory factor was the death of Domitian in 96. It is argued that Martial's excessive flattery of him (on which see Chapter 4) might have made him feel unwelcome in the changed atmosphere under Nerva (96-8), a comparative nonentity chosen by the Senate as a man certain to look after its own interests, and Trajan, born in Spain and hardly known at Rome, but chosen by Nerva for his military distinction and business-like efficiency. However, the new situation seems to have caused no problems for men who had behaved far worse.

In the penultimate poem of Book X Martial tells his fellow-townsmen at Bilbilis that he is their glory, as Catullus was that of his native Verona, and asks them to welcome him back – threatening that otherwise he may return to Rome. In the final poem he sends his book there, as companion to his friend Flavius, and asks it to

1. Chapter 1. The Life of Martial

greet the friends he has not seen for 34 years, though they are now few, and to remind Flavius to find him a pleasant and reasonably-priced place of retirement, where he can grow lazy.

The younger Pliny tells us in a letter written after Martial's death (3.21), addressed to the otherwise unknown Cornelius Priscus, that he had given him money for the journey. The letter is our only substantial piece of external evidence for Martial's life and character. It provides an interesting example of the kind of reward a wealthy man like Pliny would feel was the natural return for verses in which he was praised.

> I hear that Valerius Martialis has died, and I am sorry. He was talented, sharp, and passionate, and in his writing he had a great deal of wit and gall and an equal amount of frankness. When he left Rome, I helped him with a contribution for his journey: this was in return for his friendship, and also for the verses which he wrote about me. It was an old custom to reward those who had written eulogies of individuals or of cities with either honours or money; however, in our own times, along with many other attractive and admirable practices, this one likewise has been conspicuous in becoming obsolete. For, since we have ceased to do things worthy of praise, we consider it bad form also to be praised.
>
> Do you ask which are the verses for which I

showed my gratitude? I should refer you to the volume itself, if I did not know some of them by heart; if these please you, you will look out the rest in the book. He addresses his Muse, and bids her seek out my house on the Esquiline, and approach it reverently [10.20]:

'But take care not to beat on his eloquent door at a time which does not belong to you: he gives up his whole days to stern Minerva, while he works to please the ears of the hundred men [the centumviral court] with work which later ages may compare even with Cicero's pages. It will be safer for you to go when the late lamps are lit: this is your hour, when the god of relaxation raves, when the rose rules, when hair drips with perfume. Then let even stiff Catos read me!'

Was I justified both in giving a most friendly send-off to the man who wrote these things about me, and in grieving now for the death of an excellent friend? For he gave me the greatest gift he could, and would have given more if he had been able. And yet what greater gift can be given to a man than glory and praise and eternity? 'But what he wrote will not last for eternity': perhaps it will not, but he wrote as if it would. Farewell.

It is ironic that, despite what Pliny says, it is Martial's works which have survived, whereas the works of Pliny by which he would most have hoped to be remembered (the

1. The Life of Martial

forensic speeches referred to in the poem which he quotes) have perished.

At first Martial found life in Spain idyllic. He had a generous benefactress called Marcella, and it was she who provided him with a house and a small estate. He wrote a rapturous poem to a friend called Juvenal (surely the future satirist), teasing him about the life he still lived at Rome (12.18). We have so little evidence for Juvenal's life that this is all the more fascinating. Gilbert Highet (who thought that Martial was 'a nasty little man') called it 'rather cruel … gloating', but it is surely affectionately humorous.

Dum tu forsitan inquietus erras
clamosa, Iuvenalis, in Subura
aut collem dominae teris Dianae,
dum per limina te potentiorum
sudatrix toga ventilat vagumque
maior Caelius et minor fatigant:
me multos repetita post Decembres
accepit mea rusticumque fecit
auro Bilbilis et superba ferro.
hic pigri colimus labore dulci
Boterdum Plateamque – Celtiberis
haec sunt nomina crassiora terris - :
ingenti fruor improboque somno
quem nec tertia saepe rumpit hora,
et totum mihi nunc repono quidquid
ter denos vigilaveram per annos.

Martial

ignota est toga, sed datur petenti
rupta proxima vestis a cathedra.
surgentem focus excipit superba
vicini strue cultus iliceti,
multa vilica quem coronat olla.
venator sequitur, sed ille quem tu
secreta cupias habere silva;
dispensat pueris rogatque longos
levis ponere vilicus capillos.
sic me vivere, sic iuvat perire.

While you are perhaps wandering about anxiously, Juvenal, in the noisy Subura [a busy street in the middle of Rome], or treading the hill of mistress Diana [the Aventine], while the sweating toga flaps you through the thresholds of the more powerful men, and both the greater and the lesser Caelian hill wear you out as you roam, so far as I'm concerned my Bilbilis, sought again after many Decembers, has welcomed me and made me a rustic, Bilbilis proud of its gold and iron. Here we idlers cultivate with pleasant labour Boterdus and Platea – these are the rather lumpish names for our Celtiberian lands. I enjoy enormous and shameful amounts of sleep, which frequently not even the third hour interrupts, and I am now making good the whole of my wakefulness over thirty years. The toga is unknown, but, when I ask, the nearest piece of clothing is given to

1. The Life of Martial

me from a broken chair. The hearth welcomes me when I get up, piled with the proud spoil of the nearby ilex-grove, which my she-bailiff crowns with many a cooking pot. The huntsman follows, and he is a man whom you would wish to have to yourself in a secluded wood. The smooth-cheeked bailiff gives their rations to the slaves, and asks permission to have his long hair cut off. This is how I am pleased to live, this is how I am pleased to die.

While still at Rome, Martial had written that the reward he wanted more than any other for his work was sleep (10.74). As both Martial and Juvenal complained, you had to be a rich man to sleep in the city, where the fact that wheeled traffic was not allowed in except at night meant that poorer people, who lived over or near the street, were kept awake by the noise. In fact Martial had claimed that, if he wanted to sleep, he had to go to his country place at Nomentum (12.57).

Before long, however, Martial became disillusioned with provincial life. He sent back his Book XII from there in 101 or 102 (an enlarged version appeared later, possibly after his death). In the preface he complains about the lack of the stimulus of literary society, and small-town scandal-mongering. Even his precious sleep was disturbed by clients calling in the early morning to seek his advice on their legal problems, described as his reason for leaving the city (12.68). Within a few years of his return – certainly by

104 – he was dead. When the news reached Rome, Pliny wrote the letter quoted above.

One can draw certain conclusions, unprovable but probable, from Martial's works. As already mentioned, he seems never to have married. It is hardly likely that 11.104, which is addressed to *uxor* (wife), is addressed to a real wife, as he reproves her in the most specific detail for her prudish refusal to indulge his taste for varieties of sexual enjoyment, culminating in sodomy. At 2.92 he comically argues that the emperor's gift of the *ius trium liberorum* would be wasted if he married – so 'goodbye, wife'. Although by no means blind to the attractions of the opposite sex, he seems to have had a preference for his own; many poems refer to boys as objects of affection. Friendship mattered greatly to him. Warm-hearted and quarrelsome, he was eternally inquisitive, but not malicious. As we have seen, he liked nothing so much as a quiet and sociable life, enjoying the sights, the gossip, and the luxuries of Rome. He never ceases to encourage his friends and readers to enjoy life while they can, and not take things too seriously.

As an example of his shrewdness and understanding of human nature, this chapter may end with his final address to his closest friend, Julius Martialis – in effect, his farewell to him on leaving Rome (12.34):

Triginta mihi quattuorque messes
tecum, si memini, fuere, Iuli,
quarum dulcia mixta sunt amaris,

1. The Life of Martial

sed iucunda tamen fuere plura;
et si calculus omnis huc et illuc
diversus bicolorque digeratur,
vincet candida turba nigriorem.
si vitare voles acerba quaedam
et tristis animi cavere morsus,
nulli te facias nimis sodalem:
gaudebis minus et minus dolebis.

If I remember rightly, you and I have had thirty-four summers together, Julius, in which the sweet has been mixed with the bitter, but all the same the pleasures were in the majority; and if every different pebble, of each colour, were separated in each direction, the white pile will outnumber the blacker one. If you want to avoid any unpleasantness and to take precautions against wretched pains of the heart, you should not make yourself too close a friend to anyone: you will be less happy, and less miserable.

2
What is an Epigram?

The most celebrated answer to this question was provided by Samuel Taylor Coleridge, in an epigram (adapted from a German poem by Wernicke) published in the *Morning Post* in 1802:

> What is an epigram? A dwarfish whole;
> Its body brevity, and wit its soul.

Similarly the *Concise Oxford Dictionary* defines it as a 'Short poem ending in a witty turn of thought'. Even a quick look at Martial's poems will show how this fails to fit a great number of them. How then did such a modern definition come about?

The word 'epigram' comes from the Greek 'epigramma', meaning an inscription. It used to be held that the earliest use was for epitaphs, but the oldest known epigrams, dating from the late eighth century BC, are both inscribed on pots, and both depend on Homer, using his metre, the hexameter. One identifies a jug as a prize for dancing, while the other refers to Nestor's cup. Later on – possibly as early as the seventh century – epigrams in elegiac couplets (hexameter plus pentameter) appear, and by the fifth century this is the commonest metre. Although the epigram is most often used either for epitaphs or for dedicatory inscriptions, there are many examples of purely literary creations, such as imaginary epitaphs. Humour is often an important element, as in Archilochus' famous four-line poem about throwing away his shield:

> One of the Saioi [a Thracian people] rejoices in my shield, which I abandoned unwillingly by the shore, a blameless weapon. But I saved myself: what do I care about that shield? Good riddance; another time I shall get one just as good.

He is playing on the idea expressed in the old story about the Spartan woman, seeing her son off to battle, who tells him to come back either with his shield or on it - i.e. dead.

Even in early epigrams there is sometimes a satirical intention; for example, an epigram by the obscure Demodocus (apparently writing in the sixth century BC): 'All Lerians are bad, not one bad but another not, all except Procles – but Procles too is a Lerian.'

The Hellenistic period was the great age of the epigram; almost all the best poets wrote them and took the genre very seriously. For those who agreed with the greatest poet of the time, Callimachus, in valuing brevity, this was not surprising. Martial himself (4.23), like Pliny, considered Callimachus the finest of Greek epigrammatists. Apart

2. What is an Epigram?

from a few discoveries on papyrus, our knowledge of Hellenistic epigram depends ultimately on the anthology, the 'garland', put together by Meleager in about 100 BC. Meleager's *Garland* may have contained as many as 1,000 poems. His selection was based on principles which have helped to shape our concept of the genre. Most are in elegiac couplets, and all are short (rarely more than eight lines). They seem to have been grouped by subject. A substantial portion consisted of erotic epigrams (heterosexual and homosexual undifferentiated) – the type for which Meleager himself was best known. By his time the elegiac couplet was virtually standard for the genre.

It is not certain whether the genre of satirical epigram as such (as opposed to occasional examples) existed before the time of the later Greek epigrammatists whose work was collected by Philip of Thessalonica in his *Garland*, published under Nero. This collection reveals the pervasive influence of rhetoric, then at its height in Rome, and the satirical epigram is now common. Its most striking exponent in Greek was Lucillius, who wrote at Rome in the generation after Philip, and was an important model for Martial.

The arrangement of the poems in the *Greek Anthology* in its present form (the *Palatine Anthology*) was made by Constantinus Cephalas in about AD 900. It is done by type, and appears to have no relationship to the way the *Garlands* were originally arranged. What appear to be Cephalas' categories include erotic poems, dedications, epitaphs, and the genres of epideictic (describing remarkable events), protreptic (moralising), sympotic (on dinner or drinking parties), and scoptic (or satirical) poems. To these can be added ecphrastic poems (describing works of art), poems of praise, and hymns and prayers.

This classification can be applied to many of Martial's epigrams, though he frequently adapts or blends them. Erotic poems are very common, dedications less so, though examples are Pudens' dedication of his boy-lover's hair (1.31) and Earinus' dedication of his mirror and hair (9.16 and 17). Epitaphs can be genuine, like those for the slave-girl Erotion (5.34 and 10.61), or for a hunting-dog (11.69), or alternatively satirical (for example, 9.29). Epideictic poems include many on incidents in the amphitheatre or circus. Protreptic epigrams reveal the serious side to Martial's art, and two celebrated examples have been quoted above (5.20; 10.47 – see pp. 19, 21). The theme of the dinner-party is one he is fond of, for example, invitation poems in which the menu is specified (5.78; 10.48; 11.52). The satirical epigram is so much Martial's speciality that illustrations need not be given. Ecphrastic poems include descriptions of villas such as that of Faustinus at Baiae (3.58), and of works of art such as a bronze statuette of Hercules (9.43). Praise of contemporaries was obviously a frequent theme: the poem about Pliny has been quoted above (10.20). An epigram in the form of a hymn is 8.8, to Janus, but more striking is the parody of a hymn at 5.24, celebrating the gladiator Hermes. The prayer-form is closely related,

2. What is an Epigram?

such as the good wishes to his friend Pudens on his marriage (4.13), and the prayer for Trajan's safe return from the Rhine (10.7).

Two recent discoveries on papyrus may have brought us a little closer to the intentions of two of the poets included in the *Greek Anthology*, but we cannot know whether even these collections were actually put together by their authors. One contains 112 poems, or fragments of poems, by Posidippus, an author of the third century BC (a contemporary of Callimachus), celebrated as an epigrammatist. He was particularly known for his poems on love and wine, but none appears in this collection. Here the poems are arranged by subject-matter, including precious stones, omens, dedications, statues, horses, shipwrecks, cures, and (perhaps) characters: the broad range is interesting. The other recently discovered papyrus contains parts of eight epigrams. As three are known to be by Nicarchus, a contemporary of Lucillius, the rest are assumed to be his too. The themes appear to be all satirical, and include pederasty, adultery, and the old man with a young wife, together with oddities such as a joke about a leaky boat and an obscene explanation of the riddle of the Sphinx. Although fascinating, especially in their variety of content, these new discoveries throw little positive light on the arrangement of books of epigrams before the time of Martial.

There is a good deal of scattered and rather scrappy evidence for a long-standing tradition of epigram in

Latin, the earliest surviving examples being the epitaphs inscribed on the tombs of the Scipio family at Rome, which are in the native metre known as the Saturnian. A few epitaphs of authors survive, implausibly attributed to the writers themselves. This is the proud boast put into the mouth of Ennius (probably by a grammarian of the second century BC):

> Nemo me lacrimis decoret nec funera fletu
>   faxit. cur? volito vivus per ora virum.

> Let no one honour me with tears, or accompany my funeral with lamentation. Why? I fly, alive, through the mouths of men.

The concise structure is remarkable: the first line states a paradox – all Romans would want to be mourned. Then comes the question why, with the emphatic reply. The form and metre come from Greek literature, but the alliteration is a Latin device.

It is most unlikely that these were real epitaphs, but at 11.90.4 Martial quotes the pentameter from the striking elegiac couplet written towards the end of the second century BC in memory of a favourite slave by Lucilius, who was regarded by Horace as the founder of the genre of satire. A few epigrams survive from around 100 BC which are certainly literary. These include two by the distinguished statesman and general Q. Lutatius Catulus, one

2. What is an Epigram?

praising the beauty of the actor Roscius, and another, based on an epigram by Callimachus, which is quoted by Gellius as an example of a poem by an early Roman about the love of boys. There are also some comic epigrams among Pompeian graffiti, which make free use of obscenity. A few other examples attack prominent men such as Julius Caesar. Suetonius (*Divus Iulius* 49.3) quotes some verses sung at Caesar's Gallic triumph by the soldiers following his chariot, referring to his supposed relationship with the king of Bithynia:

> Gallias Caesar subegit, Nicomedes Caesarem:
> ecce Caesar nunc triumphat qui subegit Gallias,
> Nicomedes non triumphat qui subegit Caesarem.

> Caesar subjugated the Gauls, Nicomedes subjugated Caesar; look! Caesar who subjugated the Gauls is now triumphing; Nicomedes who subjugated Caesar is not triumphing.

Catullus' close friend Calvus attacked Pompey:

> Magnus, quem metuunt omnes, digito caput uno
>   scalpit: quid credas hunc sibi velle? virum.

> Magnus, whom everyone fears, scratches his head with one finger. What would you think he is after? A man.

Scratching the head with one finger, to avoid disturbing one's coiffure, was regarded as a sign of a homosexual.

Catullus was for Martial his most significant predecessor. He tells us that his fondest ambition would be to be placed second to him (10.78.16; see also 5.5; 7.99; 10.103). Many people think of Catullus as a 'lyric' poet, so that it may seem surprising to find him categorised by Martial (in the Preface to Book I) as an epigrammatist. However, there is no reason why many, or even most, of his shorter poems (1-60 and 69-116) should not be considered as epigrams. One of the most famous (85) is a perfect example of the genre:

> Odi et amo. quare hoc faciam fortasse requiris.
>   nescio, sed fieri sentio et excrucior.

> I hate and I love. Perhaps you ask why I do this. I don't know, but I feel it happening and am tormented.

As in the Ennius poem quoted above, we have a paradoxical statement, followed by the question why, and then the answer, itself containing an antithesis.

In the preface to his Book I, Martial puts Catullus first in a list of predecessors who indulged in 'playful frankness of vocabulary, or, in other words, the language of epigram'. In the first part of this preface (which will be discussed more fully later), Martial insists that he never attacks real people, not even under pseudonyms. In this, however, he differed

2. What is an Epigram?

from Catullus (whose most distinguished victims were Julius Caesar and his chief engineer Mamurra – see poems 29 and 93), the most obvious reason being that the changed political and social circumstances ruled out such attacks.

So far as Martial was concerned, the chief importance of the other epigrammatists who wrote between the time of Catullus and his own was their use of obscenity. So, for example, at 11.20 he actually quotes a six-line epigram by 'Caesar Augustus', which he praises for its *Romana simplicitas* – 'Roman frankness'. The poem was written when Augustus was a young man, and attacks Antony's wife Fulvia with remarkably obscene insults. In the preface to Book I he names three obscure authors after Catullus (Marsus, Pedo and Gaetulicus), and he mentions the first two again several times.

In fact, the writing of epigrams was clearly by now a frequent pastime at Rome. In one of his letters the younger Pliny refers to his own small-scale verse compositions, and justifies his frivolity, apparently involving freedom of language (and surprising given the priggish tone he adopts in his letters), by reference to an astonishing list of other authors. This includes more than twenty literary men, senators and emperors, among them Ennius, Virgil, Cicero, Seneca, Brutus, Sulla, Julius Caesar, Augustus, Tiberius, and Nerva.

In the preface to the first book, Martial anticipates criticism on the two scores of personal attack and obscenity, but it becomes clear that he also had to face complaints about the length and metre of some of his poems. So far as length is concerned, it is obvious that inscriptions should be kept as brief as possible. The anonymous author of *The Arte of English Poesie* (1589) argued that epitaphs should be 'in few verses, pithie, quicke and sententious for the passer to peruse, and judge upon without any long tariaunce'. As has been pointed out, the liking of the Hellenistic poets for epigram must have been due to their emphasis on the importance of brevity. On the other hand, the longest epigram by Callimachus himself runs to sixteen lines, and an epigram by the second-century BC poet Antipater of Sidon has twenty-four.

It is only in the *Garland of Philip* (see above) that we first find a pedantic insistence on brevity. Poems by the obscure minor poets Parmenion and Cyrillus (whose dates are unknown) state that epigrams should not exceed four, or maybe six, lines. It has been suggested that these poets were reacting against a tendency to write long epigrams prevalent at Rome among poets following the example of Catullus (whose poem 76 runs to 26 lines) and works such as the *Catalepton* attributed to Virgil.

Martial's longest epigrams are 3.58 (51 lines) and 1.49 (42 lines – quoted above, p. 23). Although Sullivan estimates the average length in the twelve 'miscellaneous' books as 7.4 lines, there are thirty-two epigrams of over twenty lines (mostly in metres other than elegiacs, at any rate up to Book VIII), and many have more than ten. (By contrast, 8.19 consists of just one line.)

2. What is an Epigram?

Similarly, Martial was criticised for writing an epigram in hexameters (6.64-5). In fact, although the elegiac couplet was the commonest metre for epigrams throughout almost the whole history of the genre, both before and during the Hellenistic period other metres were quite freely used. In justification Martial might well have pointed to the example of Catullus. However Catullus himself might have classified his poems (and we have no way of knowing this, apart from his reference to *nugae* (trifles) in the prefatory hendecasyllabic poem), Martial clearly regarded all Catullus's shorter poems as epigrams – including the famous poem about the *passer* (sparrow). It would be a great advantage if we had the poems of Catullus in their original arrangement. Some scholars think that we do, but the placing of all the non-elegiac short poems first (with the prefatory poem in hendecasyllables necessarily put at the beginning), and the short poems in elegiacs last, and the longer poems in between, seems most unlikely to be the work of Catullus himself. The example of Martial suggests that the short poems would have been placed together, with the different metres providing variety. However, it is possible that traces remain of the original arrangement: the two poems about kisses, addressed to Lesbia (5 and 7), are separated by one other poem, which would anticipate Martial's tendency to put two poems on the same subject, not side by side, but not too far apart (see below). A lack of dogmatism in Martial's time concerning the classification of short poems is shown by the younger Pliny, who, in the letter referred to above, says that his short poems can be called epigrams, or idylls, or eclogues, or *poematia* (short poems) – he himself calls them simply by their metre, hendecasyllables.

We come back to the question, raised at the beginning of this chapter, of how the epigram came to be defined in the way Coleridge described it. The answer is that Martial brought this type of epigram to such a pitch of perfection that it has come to seem the ideal form. This was admitted by J.W. Mackail, who far preferred the poets of the *Greek Anthology* to Martial, who, he wrote in 1895, 'gave a meaning to the word epigram from which it is only now beginning to recover', setting 'a narrow and rather disastrous type for later literature'.

In a famous discussion, the eighteenth-century German dramatist Gotthold Ephraim Lessing claimed that epigrams separate into two parts: 'in the first of these our attention is directed to some particular object, our curiosity is aroused concerning some specific subject, whereas in the second our attention reaches its mark and our curiosity receives an explanation'. He called the first part 'Erwartung' (expectation) and the second 'Aufschluss' (conclusion). A perfect example would be 1.10:

Petit Gemellus nuptias Maronillae
et cupit et instat et precatur et donat.
adeone pulchra est? immo foedius nil est.
quid ergo in illa petitur et placet? tussit.

2. What is an Epigram?

Gemellus wants to marry Maronilla, and longs and presses and begs and gives her presents. Is she then so beautiful? No – nothing could be uglier. So what is it that makes her sought after and attractive? She coughs.

Our expectation is aroused by the paradox of Gemellus' frantic desire to marry an ugly woman, but the explanatory 'conclusion', expressed in the final word (and emphasised by the repeated 't' sound, and the 'limping' metre) implies that she is consumptive, and (we are left to assume) rich. In fact, Martial rarely employs the device of putting the point into the final word, to avoid its becoming wearisome if over-used.

It is obvious that Lessing's definition fits only a limited number even of Martial's epigrams. He would have approved of the much less dogmatic definition expressed by Lessing's contemporary, the romantic poet Friedrich Gottlieb Klopstock (1724-1803), as the preface to his own epigrams:

> Bald ist das Epigramm ein Pfeil,
>   Trifft mit der Spitze;
>   Ist bald ein Schwert,
>   Trifft mit der Schärfe;
> Ist manchmal auch (die Griechen liebten's so)
> Ein klein Gemäld', ein Strahl, gesandt
> Zum Brennen nicht, nur zum Erleuchten.

Martial

Sometimes the epigram is an arrow – it hits with its point; sometimes it is a sword – it hits with its sharpness; it is often also (the Greeks liked it so) a small picture, a ray of light, sent not to burn but to illuminate.

3
Martial and the Epigram

Martial's reasons for confining himself to the genre of epigram have already been discussed. Nothing could be clearer from his work than his dislike of all that was pretentious and hypocritical, and this humble genre allowed him to be true to himself. A large proportion of his epigrams are satirical. They attack vice, or absurdity, or socially aggravating behaviour, and the victims are particularised with names. Had these been identifiable as real people, he would have incurred risk, since emperors generally discouraged such attacks, not just on themselves, as one might expect, but on any citizens. Martial uses the substantial preface to his first book, written mostly in prose to distinguish it from the rest of the work, in the first place to stress the fact that his poems 'have their fun without infringing the respect due even to the lower class of persons'. He speaks out particularly strongly against any 'spiteful interpreter' who might wish to substitute real names for the fictitious ones. It is interesting to compare Juvenal: writing in the tradition of satire, he felt obliged to attack real people, but he claims that it would have been far too dangerous to attack the living, and so he targets dead individuals instead.

There is more to this than a mere desire to keep out of trouble. It was also alien to Martial's fundamental good nature. He would have agreed with the rule laid down by his fellow-Spaniard Quintilian: 'a laugh is won at too high a price if it costs the loss of a good character' (*Institutio Oratoria*, Preface). There was, however, a positive gain on the literary front. Martial's attacks might have gained in topicality and fire for his contemporary readers had the individuals been named or recognisable, but such attacks tend to lose their interest when readers are unfamiliar with the victims. Martial's generalised attacks gain a timelessness and breadth of application which doubtless helped them to appeal to a wide readership, and to survive the years.

Martial goes on in his preface to deal with obscenity. After referring, as has been mentioned, to his Latin predecessors, and especially Catullus, in a characteristically blunt way, he points out that anyone who is 'read right through' writes like this, while suggesting that anyone who dislikes 'plain Latin' should just read the preface – or even just the title. He ends by making a clever reference to a celebrated story about the younger Cato, the great Stoic hero. When he came into the theatre at the time of the Ludi Florales (shows in honour of the goddess Flora), the audience was so embarrassed that it did not dare to make its traditional demand for the actresses to strip naked. When this was pointed out to Cato, he left the theatre, to great applause. This is regarded by Valerius Maximus as a

3. Martial and the Epigram

tribute to Cato's virtue, but Martial slyly asks whether, since Cato must have known well what usually happened, he only entered the theatre so as to make a grand exit.

Obscenity has become so much the defining characteristic of Martial that its real pervasiveness has been absurdly exaggerated. He goes no further than Aristophanes, Catullus, or Juvenal. It is worth noting that, when the French lawyer Vincent Collesson produced the 'Delphin edition' (for the use of the Dauphin) in 1680, he relegated only 150 'obscene' epigrams, out of a total of more than 1,500, to an appendix at the end – a bizarre solution which, as Byron pointed out in *Don Juan* (I.44) 'saves in fact the trouble of an index' (see also p. 112). More tender-minded editors have doubled Collesson's total.

We have stronger sensibilities today, and may frankly admit that many of Martial's funniest poems are to be found among the 'obscene' ones. Much the most uninhibited book is XI, which celebrates the Saturnalia (the December festival of freedom and fun) and the accession of Nerva, which means that they can be properly (or improperly) enjoyed.

A striking feature of Martial's obscenity is his use of vulgar language (avoided, in contrast, by Juvenal). In his book *The Latin Sexual Vocabulary*, J.N. Adams remarks (p. 7): 'that Martial could use direct terminology in literary epigram (unlike his predecessors in Greek) and still claim that his work might be amusing to sophisticated readers (including women) is something of a curiosity', and explains that 'to some extent he was expecting to amuse by being deliberately outrageous ... The Romans (and not only men) clearly enjoyed blatant sexual language on special occasions.' Adams draws particular attention to Martial's claim that his epigrams can be enjoyed even by respectable women, concluding that 'he is a special case' who 'writes with the attitude of one deliberately flouting conventional attitudes' (p. 217).

The biggest problem for the author of a collection of short poems is how to arrange them so as to achieve as much variety as possible, and prevent the reader from becoming wearied. As Martial himself says, 'It's easy to write pretty epigrams, but hard to write a book' (7.85.3f.). Apart from the immense variety of his subject-matter, he counters this in part by his use of different metres. Almost three-quarters of the epigrams are in elegiac couplets, but the others are scattered about so artfully that they succeed in giving the impression of variety. The next commonest metre is the hendecasyllable (line of eleven syllables), particularly noted for its use by Catullus, though much used by other authors too (e.g. Pliny, as mentioned above). This accounts for about twenty per cent of the poems in Books I-XII. Third comes the scazon, or 'limping iambic', associated by tradition with invective. This is used for about six per cent of the poems. Occasionally Martial uses another metre: for example, 1.49 (for which see above) is in a combination of alternating iambic trimeters and dimeters, the choice

3. Martial and the Epigram

explained by the fact that the epigram is based on a poem by Horace (the second Epode) in the same metre. In his use of the various metres Martial avoids the extremes of either rigidity or licence; he pursues the middle course that one would expect of so well-tempered a writer.

Martial takes great trouble over the arrangement of the poems within each book. Variety could also be achieved in subject-matter. On the other hand, interrelationships could also play a significant role. The beginning of a book is obviously the most important place, and poems put here are most likely to be seen by the casual reader: hence the tendency to place here poems which praise a patron – often the emperor. Five of the fifteen books have prefaces in prose, a practice which Martial himself sends up in the preface to Book II. On the other hand, to put all the poems praising the emperor together might seem excessive, and so they can be placed at intervals throughout the book.

Martial likes to write groups of poems on the same subject (usually referred to by the term 'cycles'). He does not place the whole group together, but puts them at fairly close intervals, so that the reader is not bored, but can still perceive the interconnections. Similarly, when Martial writes two poems on the same subject, they are usually placed, not side by side, but not too far apart. On the other hand, it can be the case that two have to be consecutive for the meaning of the second to be comprehensible. 6.64, a poem in 32 hexameters, is followed by one of three elegiac couplets in which Martial replies to a man who criticises him for using the hexameter for epigram. Long poems are often followed by short ones. Sometimes a humorous poem interrupts a more solemn sequence. Occasionally the interrelationships are subtle: for example, 5.64 refers to imperial mausolea, which might seem tactless, but the next poem asks the gods to grant Domitian long life.

Only too often Martial is read in the form of a 'selection'. This makes it impossible to appreciate his skill in arranging his books, and some clever tricks go by the board. For example, in Book III poem 68 tells the matron that so far the book has been written for her, but from here on it contains 'naked males', and calls a prick a prick. Martial ends by saying that the matron, who was getting bored, will now read the book through to the end. And in poem 86 he catches out the 'chaste woman', who is still reading.

With the ironic self-depreciation which is typical of his persona, Martial several times points out that his poems are not all equally good (1.16), arguing that the only entirely consistent book is a bad one (7.90). Similarly, when his publisher John Murray told Byron that half of *Don Juan* was 'very good', he replied 'You are wrong; for, if it were, it would be the finest poem in existence'. Martial suggests that his reader should pick and choose, skimming over the poems which are not to his taste (6.65; 11.106; 14.2).

The influence of rhetoric, in which all educated men were trained, was at its height, and some poems show the unfortunate effect of cleverness divorced from reality. One

3. Martial and the Epigram

example (4.18) deals with a boy whose throat was pierced by an icicle falling from an aqueduct (which sounds implausible enough), and the 'point' is that the 'blade' melts in the wound: can even water cut throats? Another (5.74) tells how the two sons of Pompey are buried, one in Asia, the other in Europe, while their father, if indeed he was buried (after his head was cut off on the beach), lies under Libyan soil: 'so great a fall could not lie in one single place'. For us the point seems frigid, but this kind of sententious stuff about historical figures was so much to contemporary taste that seven anonymous epigrams dealing with the same subject probably derive from it (*Anthologia Latina*, ed. D.R. Shackleton Bailey, 396-9 and 452-4).

It is amusingly characteristic of Martial that he even anticipates the work of his later editors. The textual critic, concerned to establish the correct text of the author, finds this poem, addressed to a good friend (7.11): 'You urge me to emend my little books, Pudens, with my pen and my own hand. O, how you admire and love me to excess, who want to possess my trifles in autograph!' He is, of course, joking: works copied from manuscript to manuscript were bound to accumulate errors. At 10.21 it is the commentators who are not wanted:

> Scribere te quae vix intellegat ipse Modestus
>   et vix Claranus, quid, rogo, Sexte, iuvat?
> non lectore tuis opus est, sed Apolline libris:
>   iudice te maior Cinna Marone fuit.

sic tua laudentur sane: mea carmina, Sexte,
   grammaticis placeant ut sine grammaticis.

Why does it please you, Sextus, to write stuff that Modestus himself and Claranus [two commentators] scarcely understand? Your books need not a reader but an Apollo [god of obscure oracles]. By your judgment Cinna was greater than Virgil. So may your poems be praised, to be sure; let my poems, Sextus, please the commentators in such a way that they have no need of commentators.

Cinna was a friend of Catullus who took nine years over the writing of a poem called *Zmyrna*, which was so obscure that within a few decades a commentary was produced.

A word should be said about the *Xenia* and *Apophoreta* (Books XIII and XIV). There is nothing quite like them elsewhere in ancient literature, and some critics have dismissed them as mere 'cracker mottoes'. This is misleading; their recent editor T.J. Leary has shown that they belong to a tradition of 'catalogue' poems, listing presents which could appropriately be sent at the Saturnalia – a type of poem which also appears in Martial's later books. Although ostensibly intended to be attached to the various gifts, they are really virtuoso performances of poetic and descriptive skill. For us they have the further advantage of providing information on an immense range of objects and activities, including

3. Martial and the Epigram

even works of literature. For example, Martial makes a sly dig at Lucan (14.194):

> Sunt quidam qui me dicant non esse poetam:
>   sed qui me vendit bybliopola putat.

There are some who say that I am not a poet, but the bookseller who sells me thinks I am.

It was Martial's firm belief that what gave his work its appeal was its reflection of real life. So, at 10.4 he writes:

> Qui legis Oedipoden caligantemque Thyesten,
>   Colchidas et Scyllas, quid nisi monstra legis?
> quid tibi raptus Hylas, quid Parthenopaeus et Attis,
>   quid tibi dormitor proderit Endymion,
> exutusve puer pinnis labentibus, aut qui
>   odit amatrices Hermaphroditus aquas?
> quid te vana iuvant miserae ludibria chartae?
>   hoc lege, quod possit dicere vita 'meum est'.
> non hic Centauros, non Gorgonas Harpyiasque
>   invenies: hominem pagina nostra sapit.
> sed non vis, Mamurra, tuos cognoscere mores
>   nec te scire: legas Aetia Callimachi.

You who read about Oedipus and Thyestes, lost in darkness [in the eclipse after his brother Tereus served up his children for him to eat], Colchian women [like Medea] and Scyllas, what do you read about except monsters? What good will the abducted Hylas do you, or Parthenopaeus or Attis, or the sleeping Endymion, or the boy stripped of his slipping feathers [Icarus], or Hermaphroditus who hates the waters which love him? How do useless mockeries of wretched paper benefit you? Read this, of which life can declare 'It's mine'. Here you will find no Centaurs, Gorgons or Harpies: my page tastes of mankind. But you don't want, Mamurra, to recognise your own character, nor to know yourself; you should read Callimachus's *Aetia* [his longest and most learned work, dealing with every sort of 'aetion', or 'origin]'.

He even weighs epigram against this sort of mythological poetry, with surprising results (4.49):

> Nescit, crede mihi, quid sint epigrammata, Flacce,
>   qui tantum lusus illa iocosque vocat.
> ille magis ludit qui scribit prandia saevi
>   Tereos aut cenam, crude Thyesta, tuam,
> aut puero liquidas aptantem Daedalon alas,
>   pascentem Siculas aut Polyphemon ovis.
> a nostris procul est omnis vesica libellis,
>   Musa nec insano syrmate nostra tumet.
> 'illa tamen laudant omnes, mirantur, adorant.'
>   confiteor: laudant illa, sed ista legunt.

3. Martial and the Epigram

> Believe me, Flaccus, a man does not know what epigrams are, if he calls them merely trivial and joking. More trivial is the author who writes about the meals of cruel Tereus or your undigested dinner, Thyestes, or Daedalus fitting liquid [wax] wings to his son, or Polyphemus feeding his Sicilian ewes. All bombast is remote from my little book, nor does my Muse swell with the crazy tragic robe. 'But those works are praised, admired, adored by everyone.' I admit: they praise those works, but these ones they read.

After all, what is the purpose of literature if not to be read? And – as we have seen – Martial tells us several times that he is read throughout the whole world, describing himself at 10.9 as 'that Martial who is known to the nations and the peoples' (but typically undercutting this by saying that he is not as well known as the horse Andraemon). More specifically, he tells us that he is read at Vienne (on the Rhone in the south of France), in Vindelicia (between the Danube and Lake Constance), in 'the North', among the frosts of Getia (Scythia, or southern Russia), and even in Britain. Confirmation of widespread familiarity with his work in later antiquity is provided by citations in inscriptions found in Germania Superior (near Châtillon-sur-Seine), Spain, the Basses Alpes, and Algeria.

Despite his pride in his achievement, Martial often presents his work as if it were mere entertainment, as at

5.16 – 'Although I could write serious works, I prefer to write entertaining ones'. Many are ready to take him at his word. A notorious example is found in the *Cambridge History of Latin Literature* (1982, p. 600), which describes him as a 'court jester', whose poetry 'never makes us think', lacking 'moral reflection'. This could not be more mistaken. At 8.3 Martial pretends to think that seven books were already too many, and had won him fame enough, but one of the Muses accuses him of ingratitude, asking whether he proposes instead to write tragedy or epic, so as to make himself hated by schoolchildren. She insists (lines 19-20):

> At tu Romano lepidos sale tinge libellos:
>   agnoscat mores vita legatque suos.

> You must dip your charming little books in Roman salt [i.e. wit], so that real life may recognise and read about its ways.

Martial regards his pointed observations on the everyday life he sees around him at Rome as having a serious moral purpose. So, at 6.60 he writes: 'My Rome praises, loves and recites my little books, and every pocket, every hand holds me. Look, someone blushes, grows pale, is stunned, gapes, hates. This is what I want: now my poems please me.' And the positive moral messages he puts across are just as serious. For example, the contrast between city and country

3. Martial and the Epigram

life was one of the corniest topics of the rhetorical schools. As a 'lifestyle choice', it had been entertainingly satirised by Horace, in his second Epode, a poem obviously very familiar to Martial, as he recalls it in his own eulogy of his homeland, 1.49 (see above). Nevertheless, for Martial himself it represented a real dilemma, which he hoped to solve by actually leaving the city. Martial's own departure must have provided his friend Juvenal with the idea for his famous third Satire, in which Umbricius, on the point of leaving Rome, tells the poet, at length and in vivid detail, why life there has become insupportable to him.

In the same way, for a provincial who had arrived at Rome without money or status, intent on a literary career, the sight of the many around him who were desperately seeking financial or social advancement, at whatever cost to their personal independence, provoked keen revulsion. Hence his reiteration of the need for people to 'live life to the full', while they still have years and health, and to enjoy the innocent pleasures readily available to them, and above all the pleasures of true friendship.

4
Martial and Domitian

Apart from his obscenity, the feature of Martial's work which contributed most to his fall from popularity in the nineteenth and twentieth centuries is his flattery of Domitian. This was described by J.W. Mackail (the biographer of William Morris) as 'gross as a mountain – it generally takes the form of comparing him with the Supreme Being, to the disadvantage of the latter' (*Latin Literature*, 1895, p. 194).

Martial had, as already mentioned, won the favour of the emperor Titus (who ruled from 79 to 81) sufficiently to be granted the privileges of a father of three children. It was believed by many that his younger brother Domitian had no great love for Titus, though on his accession he ratified the grants he had made. Nevertheless Martial published (though only in Book II) a poem asking Domitian to renew his own grant. Although (as mentioned above) we do not know which of the two gave him his titular tribunate, and so the right to equestrian rank, at the least this makes it clear how dependent he was on the emperor's favour. We have seen that the *Liber Spectaculorum* was probably written to celebrate shows put on by Domitian, and the so-called Books XIII and XIV, published two or three years after his accession, also contain compliments to him, but in Book I he plays a greater role. At 1.4 Martial asks him, should he 'happen upon my books by chance', to read them in a relaxed state of mind, and the next poem puts a humorous retort into the emperor's mouth – a liberty which he never repeated. The book contains a 'cycle' of seven poems dealing with a spectacle put on by the emperor in which a lion allowed a hare to jump in and out of its jaws. This miracle is attributed to Domitian's godlike power over animals, a power often attributed to rulers (compare, for example, the liking for lions of James I, Mussolini, and Haile Selassie), and he is indeed (as often) compared with Jupiter – the comparison which Mackail found so disgusting. This kind of adulation continues to feature in succeeding books, with the curious exception of Book III – perhaps Martial felt it less necessary to flatter the emperor when out of Rome.

Martial clearly felt that he was presented with a problem by Domitian's assumption of the 'perpetual censorship' in 85. This was an ancient Republican magistracy, whose duties were not just to draw up the 'census' of citizens, but also to guard public morals, with the right to strike off offending senators and knights. Its most famous holder was the elder Cato, the ideal of ancient Roman morality. During the first century BC the office became a mere sinecure, until Domitian appointed himself. His enemies saw this as evidence of his preposterous hypocrisy, but

4. Martial and Domitian

there is no good reason to doubt his sincerity. In the first book Martial tells the emperor that 'censorship can permit harmless fun', and, although Book VI contains, near the beginning, several poems specifically referring to the emperor's censorship, nevertheless it also contains a fair number of 'obscene' poems. However, its predecessor, Book V, is remarkable in containing none, and there is a poem explaining that this is done as a tribute to Domitian, to spare his blushes. This seems at odds with Martial's defence of his freedom of speech at 1.35, where he writes that 'it is the rule established for humorous poems that they cannot entertain unless they titillate', and asks that his books should not be 'castrated'. The explanation for the character of Book V must be that it represented an attempt to ingratiate himself further with the emperor. Book VIII is also free from obscenity, which in this case is probably due to its having been formally dedicated to Domitian.

It appears that Martial's flattery of the emperor was not as successful as he might have hoped. There is no reason to suppose that he was close to him. For example, at 9.18 he asks permission for a private water-supply to his house; the fact that he never published a poem acknowledging receipt of the privilege is usually taken to show that he did not get it. One poet who certainly did was Statius, a much more 'serious' poet, author of epic poems on Greek myths. Statius' flattery of Domitian, in his shorter poems, goes a good deal further than Martial's, and he received rewards which Martial apparently did not – for example, an invitation to dinner. Statius gives a drooling account of an imperial dinner-party at which he was present (*Silvae* 4.2) – fancy seeing the ruler of the world lying down! Martial himself does not seem to have been so honoured, despite his broad hint at 9.91: 'If the inviter [a special slave] of Caesar and the inviter of Jupiter were to summon me to dinner to different heavens, and the heavenly stars were closer, but the Palatine further off, I should give this reply to be carried back to those above: "Seek who may prefer to be the guest of the Thunderer; see, my Jupiter keeps me on earth".' Domitian's palace can be called 'the heavens' because its new banqueting hall had a ceiling decorated with stars. Although this is one of Martial's most extreme manifestations of adulation, this is diminished by the joke in the final lines, which play on the idea that to be the guest of Jupiter is to be dead.

It should be noted that Martial's probable earlier association with prominent Stoics such as Seneca may have made him less acceptable, though at 1.8 he praises the Stoic Decianus for not carrying his principles to such lengths that he has to commit suicide, a martyrdom associated with the Stoic opposition to autocracy in the reign of Nero. Similarly the senator and historian Tacitus praised his father-in-law Agricola (the governor of Britain) for not provoking Domitian by a 'useless display of liberty'. At 4.40 Martial publishes a poem lauding 'Senecas and Pisos', and praising the courage of Thrasea, a Stoic ordered to commit suicide by Nero.

4. Martial and Domitian

This is his last such reference: as Domitian's reign went on it would have been more and more tactless to keep them up.

There was a tradition of adulation in which the deification of the person flattered was a normal element – hence the official recognition as gods of the 'good' emperors. A remarkable example is the preface to Lucan's epic *Bellum Civile*, written before he fell out with Nero. Martial calls Domitian *dominus et deus* (lord and god – first at 5.8), a form of address on which Suetonius (13.2) says that he insisted. Juvenal, however, writing in the reign of Trajan (of whom Martial says that he will not call him *dominus et deus* – 10.72.3) makes fun of this kind of flattery: Domitian is delighted to be told that the giant turbot 'wanted to be caught', for 'when power is praised as equal to the gods, there is nothing which it cannot believe about itself' (4.70-1).

Some modern writers have attempted to 'rescue' Martial's reputation by arguing that, when one reads between the lines, his flattery of Domitian is actually ironic, but this fails to carry any conviction. The very fact that Quintilian (9.2.65-7) describes as a well-known technique of the rhetorical schools the saying of something while being understood to mean the opposite (and he refers particularly to the criticism of tyrants) makes it even less likely. It would have been insane for a man in Martial's social position to court the unnecessary risks which would have followed.

It needs to be taken into consideration that Domitian is not now regarded as having been the vicious tyrant that Roman historians, and Juvenal, were so keen to portray. His reputation as a 'bad emperor' (the term – reminiscent of Sellar and Yeatman's classification of kings in *1066 and All That* – goes back to Tacitus) was due largely to the hatred of the senatorial class, which he treated with paranoid severity, but he was conspicuously successful in ensuring the peace and good government of the Empire, and pleased the ordinary people of Rome by his shows and public buildings. His shows have already been mentioned. And even the fiercely hostile Suetonius admitted that 'he constantly put on magnificent and expensive spectacles, not only in the amphitheatre, but in the circus' (4.1). The shows were the principal means by which an emperor could present himself to his people, and at which the people could (and did) express their opinions to him.

Suetonius also mentions Domitian's building programme (15), another means of winning popular favour, and one for which he is today highly commended. Its chief achievements were the rebuilding of the most important temple at Rome, that of Capitoline Jupiter, which had been destroyed by fire during the civil strife of AD 69, on a lavish scale, with a portico of Pentelic marble, gold-plated doors, and gilded tiles on the roof (Martial refers to the rebuilding at 9.3.7 and 13.74), and the magnificent and innovative new palace on the Palatine

4. Martial and Domitian

Hill, which served as the imperial residence for several centuries. Martial praises its architect, Rabirius, claiming that he would be worthy to rebuild the temple of Zeus at Olympia (7.56). Domitian's activities saw about fifty buildings newly erected or restored – a record surpassed only by Augustus. Many had been destroyed in the fire under Nero (64), or in the civil war of 69. Sometimes he has lost the credit for a new building because of his *damnatio memoriae*, a notable example being the so-called Forum Nervae, or Transitorium, between Vespasian's Temple of Peace and the Forum of Augustus, which included a temple to Domitian's patron Minerva. Other notable structures included the Stadium in the Campus Martius, whose outline is represented by the Piazza Navona, and the Arch of Titus. He is also said by the hostile Suetonius (13.2) to have built so many arches to himself that a wag wrote on one '*arci*', not the plural of *arcus* (which is *arcus*), but the Greek word *arkei*, 'that's enough', but few are known of, though one, celebrating the emperor's victories in the North, is praised by Martial at 8.65: it had two golden statues of Domitian, driving chariots drawn by elephants.

In recent years his reputation has been partly rehabilitated. He seems to have been genuinely interested in literature (though Suetonius denies it). His dry sense of humour is revealed by, for example, his remark that no one ever believed that a conspiracy had been formed against an emperor until he was assassinated.

Martial

It certainly does Martial no credit that, after Domitian was indeed eventually assassinated, he heartily abused him as a lecherous tyrant. However, the Senate had decreed that Domitian should suffer what is now referred to as *damnatio memoriae* (condemnation of his memory), which involved the removal of his name from all public inscriptions, and the destruction of his imagery, as if to pretend he had never existed, so that Martial was simply following the official line. The comparison with his successors, first Nerva and then Trajan, could be much to their advantage, and Martial was quick to follow up this opportunity. He should not be blamed too much for knowing on which side his bread was buttered, and it is worth remembering that the tediously respectable Pliny, in his grovelling Panegyric on Trajan, wrote that it was the duty of loyal citizens to show their love of 'good' emperors by attacking 'bad' ones.

Martial's was by no means the only age when obsequious adulation of monarchs was regarded as normal. One can compare the lavishly fanciful eulogies addressed to Elizabeth I by poets and other writers. And the Guildhall at Windsor bears the inscription, dated 1707:

> Arte tua, sculptor, non est imitabilis Anna:
>   Annae vis similem sculpere – sculpe deam.

> Anne cannot be imitated by your art, sculptor. If you wish to carve someone similar to Anne, carve a goddess.

4. *Martial and Domitian*

It has to be said that the statue above represents a distinctly podgy human rather than a divine being.

More specifically relevant is Ben Jonson's 'To the Ghost of Martial':

> Martial, thou gav'st far nobler epigrams
> > To thy Domitian, than I can my James;
> But in my royal subject I pass thee.
> > Thou flattered'st thine, mine cannot flattered be.

5

Martial and Roman Social Life

Even in the nineteenth century, when Martial was regarded as a trivial and rather disgusting writer, he was acknowledged to throw a brilliant light on Roman social life. For example, in 1874 the Catalan painter Marian Fortuny Marsal (father of the better known painter of the same name) wrote: 'I have just been reading Martial, and he pleases me greatly, apart from the obscenity. What curious stuff on the habits and intimate life of the Romans! I have found there subjects for magnificent pictures, and I find it astonishing that painters have not made use of these authors to give their works the character of antiquity'. (Unfortunately Fortuny could not follow this up as he died that year.)

Martial's desire to reflect real life in his poems has already been mentioned (p. 57), and they have generally been found as illuminating and entertaining a source as Fortuny found them. It would be a mistake always to take them at face value. Martial may have some kind of reason to reshape, or even invent, his material to suit the purpose of the moment. Often his subjects are taken from the literary tradition.

Martial

Take, for example, his attacks on old women, represented as desperate for sex, and using every means to try to appear younger than they are. It would be a waste of time to try to find evidence for this as a contemporary phenomenon, as the topic was a stock one, going back to Greek Old Comedy, and commonly found in epigram – especially in the *Garland of Philip*. A well-known Latin example is Horace's Satire on the witch Canidia (1.8). To us, jokes about lack of teeth, or hair, or other forms of 'ugliness', are tasteless, but in the ancient world they must have been widely enjoyed. Old men are mocked too, especially for sexual impotence.

A genuine cause for complaint may underlie his attacks on the incompetence of doctors, although they too were a popular subject in comedy and satirical epigram. 1.47 is a typical example:

> Nuper erat medicus, nunc est vispillo Diaulus:
>   quod vispillo facit, fecerat et medicus.

> Diaulus was recently a doctor, but is now an undertaker. What he does as an undertaker is the same as what he did as a doctor.

Sometimes the doctor does not actually kill his patients, but merely leaves them worse off than they were. Most doctors at Rome were Greek, but even scientific writers agree that many were ignorant. One is reminded of the

5. Martial and Roman Social Life

elder Cato's warning to his son that the Greeks had sworn to kill off all the 'barbarians' by means of medicine, and that they charged fees so as to win confidence (Pliny, *Natural History* 29.14).

A profession rarely found as the subject of satirical literature is that of the auctioneer. This was despised, as it involved not only money-making, but also vulgar public display. It was certainly profitable: at 5.56 Martial advises the father of a thick son to make him an auctioneer or an architect, and at 6.8 commends the sagacity of a father who marries his daughter, not to any of the two praetors, four tribunes, seven lawyers, and ten poets who sought her hand, but to an auctioneer. 6.66 relates to a tradition of funny stories whose joke depended on the stupidity of the protagonist: an auctioneer selling a dubious girl wants to prove her purity, and kisses her several times, with the result that a man making a very low bid withdrew. At 1.85 the auctioneer is not so much stupid as excessively fond of the jokes which were the stock-in-trade of his profession: selling a suburban estate, he points out that the owner is not selling because he is in debt, but just because he lost his slaves, his herd and his crops – the result being that no one will buy it.

Lawyers are attacked for their inability to speak, an absurdity found also in Greek epigrams which play on the idea of an orator so silent that you cannot tell the difference between him and a statue of himself (and lawyers liked to have statues of themselves set up – see below). At 1.97

Naevolus only speaks when everyone is shouting, while at 8.7 Cinna demands 'four water-clocks' (which measured the length of speeches), but utters only nine words in the ten hours. The illogical absurdity of an orator who cannot speak recalls recent authors of Greek epigram such as Lucillius, who often push hyperbole into the realm of the surreal, as in the case of the man so thin that, when he plays the trumpet, he disappears down it.

There is a very personal and local flavour to Martial's attacks on schoolmasters. The worst thing about them is the noise they make, all the more annoying because they start so early in the morning. 9.68 is a bitter attack:

> Quid tibi nobiscum est, ludi scelerate magister,
>   invisum pueris virginibusque caput?
> nondum cristati rupere silentia galli:
>   murmure iam saevo verberibusque tonas.
> tam grave percussis incudibus aera resultant,
>   causidicum medio cum faber aptat equo:
> mitior in magno clamor furit amphitheatro,
>   vincenti parmae cum sua turba favet.
> vicini somnum – non tota nocte – rogamus:
>   nam vigilare leve est, pervigilare grave est.
> discipulos dimitte tuos. vis, garrule, quantum
>   accipis ut clames, accipere ut taceas?

What have you to do with us, criminal schoolmaster, hated by boys and girls? The crested cocks have not

5. Martial and Roman Social Life

yet broken the silence, but you are already making a noise with savage mumbling and blows. The bronze resounds as loudly when anvils are struck as the smith fits the lawyer to the middle of a horse [an equestrian statue]; a milder shout rages in the great amphitheatre when his fans support the conquering gladiator. We neighbours do not ask for sleep for the whole night, for lying awake is a light matter, but being awake all night is a serious business. Dismiss your pupils. Do you want, you talkative man, to receive the same amount you get to shout so as to keep quiet?'

Similarly at 5.84 the schoolmaster is 'loud-voiced', and at 8.3 he is 'swollen up with harsh voice', while at 9.29 a witch is so noisy that she could outdo 'the curly-headed gang of the early-morning schoolmaster'. We have already seen how Martial valued his sleep, but he is also moved by compassion for the children. At 10.62 he asks the master to spare them, so as to win their affection. The leather whips and the hateful rods should rest from July to October. He ends with the characteristically wise dictum: 'If boys are in good health in the summer [when Rome was notoriously unhealthy], they are learning enough'.

Martial had a genuine affection for children, and, as for so many childless Romans, the offspring of his slaves gave him much pleasure. The most conspicuous example was Erotion ('little Eros'), whose death in her sixth winter he commemorates in three epigrams. Two appear in Book V.

In the first (34) he asks his dead parents to look after her in the underworld, while in the second (37) he praises her with an exotic list of comparisons which inspired Ben Jonson's lines in *A Celebration of Charis*:

> Have you seene but a bright Lillie grow,
> > Before rude hands have touched it?
> Ha' you mark'd but the fall o' the Snow
> > Before the soyle hath smutch'd it?
> Ha' you felt the wooll o' the Bever?
> > Or Swans Downe ever?
> Or have smelt o' the bud o' the Brier?
> > Or the Nard in the fire?
> Or have tasted the bag of the Bee?
> O so white! O so soft! O so sweet is she!

The last lines of Martial's epigram introduce a 'friend' who criticises him for mourning a little slave-girl, when he has lost his noble wife. He is sarcastically reminded that his wife left him twenty million sesterces – the implication being that he had married her for her money. Some years later (10.61) Martial published a charming epitaph for Erotion, asking whoever in future will own his land to continue to make offerings at her grave.

Martial gives an extraordinarily vivid picture of life in the streets of Rome at 1.41. This is an attack on a man who thinks he is *urbanus* – possessing the smartness and wit of a resident of the 'City', as opposed to the clumsy rusticity

5. Martial and Roman Social Life

of the countryman. Martial, however, tells him that he is no more 'urbane' than any of a long list of low-life characters – the home-born slave (encouraged by his affectionate master to be cheeky), the hawker who exchanges sulphur matches for broken glass, the seller of boiled chick-peas, the snake-charmer, the slaves of salt-merchants, the hoarse cook with his steaming sausages, the rotten urban poet (author no doubt of 'Pasquinades', if not of graffiti), the impresario of a troupe of Spanish belly-dancers, the facetious old queer. All of these indulge in noisy witticism, and we are reminded of the eighteenth-century 'Cries of London', and even of the world of Henry Mayhew.

Bathing was such an important element in Roman social life that it is not surprising that it often features in Martial's work. Every free Roman would bathe daily, accompanied by one or more slaves, and he could choose from a wide variety of establishments, from the great imperial *thermae*, and luxurious private suites, to neighbourhood baths, some of which provided dubious extra services. At 1.59 Martial contrasts the baths at the fashionable resort of Baiae, on the Bay of Naples, with its natural hot springs, and the badly-lit baths run at Rome by private entrepreneurs. Best of all, according to Martial (and his contemporary Statius), were the private baths of their patron Claudius Etruscus, with their bright light, lavish marbles, and clear water; he tells Oppianus that if he does not experience these baths he will die unwashed (6.42).

The baths did not just offer facilities for washing the body. They had areas for taking exercise, whether by running, swimming, or playing games, and they were decorated with works of art, and even sometimes equipped with libraries. They were in effect the social centres of the Roman world. It is hardly surprising that they provide plenty of opportunities for writing about sex. They served as picking-up places for men:

> Audieris in quo, Flacce, balneo plausum,
> Maronis illic esse mentulam scito.

> If, Flaccus, you hear applause in a bath, you must know that Maro's penis is there (9.33).

But mixed bathing was, if not universal, at any rate common, and provided endless comic situations. J.P.V.D. Balsdon's idea that bathing dresses were worn is mistaken, as is shown by 3.51:

> Cum faciem laudo, cum miror crura manusque,
>   dicere, Galla, soles 'nuda placebo magis',
> et semper vitas communia balnea nobis.
>   numquid, Galla, times ne tibi non placeam?

> When I praise your face, when I admire your legs and hands, you always say, Galla, 'I'll please you more when I'm naked', but you always avoid having a bath

5. Martial and Roman Social Life

along with me. Is it, Galla, that you're afraid I might not please you?'

3.72, beyond the point in that book where the 'matrons' are told to stop reading (see above), develops the theme in a far more explicit way. Then there were the voyeurs, for example (11.63):

Spectas nos, Philomuse, cum lavamur,
et quare mihi tam mutuniati
sint leves pueri subinde quaeris.
dicam simpliciter tibi roganti:
pedicant, Philomuse, curiosos.

You look at us, Philomusus, when we are washing ourselves, and often ask why I have smooth-skinned slaves who are so well endowed. Since you ask, I'll tell you frankly: Philomusus, they bugger the inquisitive.

A less predictable type of social centre was the public lavatory. These had numerous seats, arranged around three sides of a rectangle, or in a semicircle. One near the Forum Caesaris at Rome even had heating. At 11.77 Martial writes:

In omnibus Vacerra quod conclavibus
consumit horas et die toto sedet,
cenaturit Vacerra, non cacaturit.

The fact that Vacerra spends hours in all the lavatories, and sits there all day, is because he's straining after a dinner invitation, not after a shit.

The desperate search for a dinner invitation on the part of the 'client' is a frequent subject for humour in Martial, exemplified by the frantic Selius at 2.14, who dashes round the town, trying every possibility, including repeated visits to a series of public and private baths. Juvenal similarly represents the client as suffering the indignity of being denied an invitation by his gluttonous patron, or, if invited, being served an inferior meal to that eaten by his host, but he castigates the client even more severely than Martial does for putting up with this servitude, claiming that *nullus iam parasitus erit* ('soon there will be no parasites left' – 1.139). The Greek word 'parasite' means a man importunate in his search for dinner invitations, and is pejorative; as so often, Juvenal's rant cuts both ways.

Food and drink are frequent subjects for Martial. Here too he favours moderation over excess. The sort of food eaten by the poor man who cannot get an invitation is represented by the boiled chickpeas described at 1.41.6 (see above) as sold in the streets, at a cost of one *as* – a small sum (there were four *asses* to the sesterce), or other food sold by hawkers, such as boiled lupin-seeds, or spicy sausages (also mentioned in 1.41). Bread, which Martial regards as the basic 'filler', usually cost two *asses* for a standard loaf for one person.

5. Martial and Roman Social Life

At 5.78 Martial invites his friend Toranius to a dinner which he calls 'starvation' – lettuces, leeks, pickled tunny with chopped eggs, cabbage, sausage and polenta, pale beans and bacon, followed by grapes, pears, and chestnuts, and finally, if Toranius is still hungry, chickpeas and lupins (which sound odd as post-prandial snacks). There is a strong element of poetical convention here, as poets often like to emphasise the simplicity of the meal they are offering. A more substantial meal is offered at 10.48 – vegetables from his estate here accompany mackerel and sow's udder, while the main course includes chicken, ham, and, as *pièce de résistance*, a kid, and fruit forms the dessert.

At the opposite extreme from the poet's 'starvation' are the gourmands who stuff themselves with boar, or exotic mushrooms (*boleti*), or expensive fish like the mullet weighing four pounds, to buy which Calliodorus sells a slave for twelve hundred sesterces (10.31). We are told that the notorious gourmet Apicius spent sixty million sesterces on food, but, reduced to his last ten million, committed suicide (3.22). A frequent target of Martial's satire (as also of Juvenal's – see above) is the host who serves food and wine to his guests which are of poorer quality than what he eats and drinks himself. So, at 1.20 Caecilianus eats *boleti* while his guests watch: Martial hopes that he will eat one like the one Claudius ate – that is, the poisoned mushroom intended to kill him. When the old-fashioned 'proper dinner' was substituted for the dole-money (see p. 98),

Martial was particularly indignant about this phenomenon (3.60). Such behaviour is not just mean, but a betrayal of the concept of friendship. Evidence that it really happened is provided by both the elder and the younger Pliny (both referring to wine). It was not, however, confined to ancient Rome. Ben Jonson praises the 'liberall boord' of Penshurst,

> Where the same beere, and bread, and self-same wine,
> That is his Lordships, shall be also mine. (*The Forrest*, 2.59-60).

George Frederick Handel was caught slipping away from his guests to drink better wine than he offered them.

Wine was something Martial clearly cared deeply about. Hence his attack (1.18) on the philistine Tucca who mixes fine old Falernian with cheap Vatican, described at 6.92 as 'poison'. Although drinking was the appropriate way to celebrate, it should not be carried to excess.

> Cum peteret seram media iam nocte matellam
>   arguto madidus pollice Panaretus,
> Spoletina data est sed quam siccaverat ipse,
>   nec fuerat soli tota lagona satis.
> ille fide summa testae sua vina remensus
>   reddidit oenophori pondera plena sui.
> miraris, quantum biberat, cepisse lagonam?
>   desine mirari, Rufe: merum biberat.(6.89)

5. Martial and Roman Social Life

When the drunken Panaretus asked for a chamber-pot, late in the middle of the night, by clicking his thumb, he was given the Spoletine flagon which he himself had drained, nor had the whole flagon been enough for him alone. With absolute faithfulness he measured out the wine of his container and gave back the full weight of his own wine-holder [i.e. his bladder]. Are you surprised that his flagon took as much as he had drunk? Don't be surprised, Rufus: he had drunk his wine neat (6.89).

The point of the joke is that the Romans normally drank wine mixed with warm water, and to drink it neat was considered greedy. At Ravenna, however, Martial claims that water is so scarce that it is more expensive than the wine.

Sex is an endlessly fascinating subject. For Martial, as for Romans in general, the active role, whether with the opposite sex or one's own, is perfectly acceptable, but the passive role for a man is disgraceful. It may come as a surprise to learn, in an age when oral sex is recommended in women's magazines, that for Martial it is definitely not all right. Oral sex performed by a man on a woman is positively dangerous, as her discharges can cause paralysis of the tongue. Lesbianism is unnatural and shocking: this was the usual attitude at Rome, so far as we can tell from literature written by men. Nevertheless, all such practices provide endless opportunities for satirical fun.

Perhaps a word should be added on orgies, still widely

believed to have been a favourite entertainment of the Romans. The disappointing truth is that there is scarcely any evidence for such activity. On the contrary, in his last book Martial shows his disapproval (12.43):

Facundos mihi de libidinosis
legisti, nimium, Sabelle, versus,
quales nec Didymi sciunt puellae
nec molles Elephantidos libelli.
sunt illic Veneris novae figurae,
quales perditus audeat fututor,
praestent et taceant quid exoleti,
quo symplegmate quinque copulentur,
qua plures teneantur a catena,
extinctam liceat quid ad lucernam.
tanti non erat esse te disertum.

Sabellus, you have read to me some excessively neat verses about lustful people, such as neither the girls of Didymus know, nor the louche books of Elephantis. In them are new patterns of love-making, such as a desperate fucker might dare to try, such activities as rent-boys provide, but keep quiet about, the intertwining by which five people are linked together, the chain by which more people still are held, and that which is permitted when the lamp has been put out. It was not worth that much for you to be an accomplished writer.

5. Martial and Roman Social Life

It is not known who 'the girls of Didymus' were, but the books of Elephantis are referred to in a notorious passage in Suetonius's life of Tiberius. It may surprise readers that Martial can show himself – by modern standards of sexual libertarianism – comparatively prudish, and it is interesting that the painted decoration in the Apodyterium (undressing room) of the recently excavated Suburban Baths at Pompeii includes erotic scenes which include a threesome, a foursome, fellatio, and cunnilinctus. This might seem to suggest that not everyone shared Martial's restraint, but the fact that each scene surmounts a painting of a box, presumably representing actual boxes for the bathers' clothing, situated below, and the numbering of these boxes from I to XVI, is thought to indicate that the scenes are merely comic ways of helping customers to remember in which box they left their clothes. (See Antonio Varone, *Eroticism in Pompeii*, Rome 2000, pp. 29f.) Even so, they hardly suggest a general revulsion at such practices.

It is another feature of the popular view of the imperial Romans that they were obsessed with public spectacles, and especially with bloodthirsty gladiatorial fights. This is not the case with Martial. It is true that his earliest work to survive is a book containing thirty-six poems about shows (the *Liber Spectaculorum*), but the reason is that it was written specifically to commemorate special shows put on by the emperor. In his later books there are comparatively few epigrams on the subject. Overall, very few deal with gladiators as such. A remarkable example is 5.24, which uses the form of a hymn to praise Hermes, 'skilled with every form of weapon', 'martial sweetheart of the age', and especially of female fans. He is described as 'expert at winning without wounding'. Poem 31 of the *Liber Spectaculorum* records what Martial describes as a unique occurrence, when the emperor gave the gladiators who were equally matched a joint discharge as reward for their skill. Contrary to what most people think about gladiators, it is clear that, not only would they themselves try to avoid shedding each other's blood, they would be admired for doing so.

Not many epigrams deal with cruelty to humans, and those which do must all refer to punishments of criminals. We find repugnant the idea of making a public spectacle of a man being savaged by a wild boar (*Liber Spectaculorum* 9), or holding his hand in a fire to imitate the Republican hero Mucius Scaevola (8.30), let alone the woman forced to have sex with a bull on the model of Pasiphae, mother of the Minotaur (*Liber Spectaculorum* 6). We are equally unlikely to approve of spectacles involving cruelty to animals, often inflicted not by humans, but by other animals. To some extent Martial was obliged to record a number of spectacles involving the death of animals, as these reflected the generosity of whoever was paying for them (usually, but not always, the emperor).

However, it is worth noting that the majority of the spectacles recorded do not involve cruelty, but instead celebrate astonishing feats of animal-training or human

5. Martial and Roman Social Life

acrobatic skill, reminding us more of the modern circus. They include the lion which allows a hare to jump in and out of its mouth (mentioned above). The remarkable list of tamed animals at 1.104 includes leopards, tigresses, stags, bears, a boar, and bisons, together with dancing elephants which remind us that Barnum and Bailey commissioned an elephant ballet from Balanchine and Stravinsky. On the other hand, some animals were valued particularly for their savagery, such as the rhinoceros (*Liber Spectaculorum* 11 and 26, in Shackleton Bailey's numbering), rarely seen at Rome, which tossed a bull, a bear, and two steers, while a buffalo, a bison and a lion were routed. This rhinoceros was so famous, and so important as a symbol of the emperor's power, that it appeared on coins of Domitian.

A spectacle which aroused at least as much passion as the shows involving gladiators and animals was chariot-racing. Martial refers to the great wealth accumulated by famous charioteers, and the huge sums spent by their rich fans on putting up equestrian statues of them (one is reminded of the statues of footballers erected outside stadiums). The races were favourite conversational topics, and betting was popular. Nero had favoured the Greens (the other teams in his time were the Blues, Whites and Reds), and Martial jokes at 11.33 about the fact that the Greens have won even more often since his death, so that their rivals cannot claim that their success was due to Nero's favour. Domitian added two new teams, the Golds and the Purples. Like football supporters, fans might wear their team's colour, and so Martial warns a man who favours the Blues or Greens that, if he wears a scarlet cloak, he may be regarded as a traitor (14.131). When Domitian goes off to take command against the Sarmatians (north of the Black Sea) in 92, Martial can think of no better way of indicating the preoccupied anxiety of the Roman people than to say that the crowd in the Circus (where the chariot races were held) does not know which well-known horse is running (7.7). Likewise, when he returns (8.11), the crowd is so busy welcoming him that no one notices that the race has started.

A curious phenomenon in Martial's Rome was legacy-hunting (called in Latin *captatio*, or 'trying to catch'). Because of the remarkable current decline in the birth-rate (something which has never been satisfactorily accounted for), there were an exceptional number of childless people, and their friends, whether real or pretended, would suck up to them in the hope of inheriting. The evils of legacy-hunting are denounced by writers from Horace onwards, and the topic is found in the *Greek Anthology*, among authors writing at Rome, as well as in Martial and Juvenal. Martial's epigram about Gemellus, who wants to marry Maronilla (1.10), has been quoted in Chapter 2, but it was rare for the legacy-hunter to go so far as to marry the old woman, and more often he would just go to her *salutatio*, like the praetors mentioned in Umbricius' tirade in Juvenal (3.129), send her presents (like Gemellus), and maybe even wipe her nose for her (Epictetus 4.1.148).

5. Martial and Roman Social Life

Martial's picture of Rome can be profitably compared with that of his friend Juvenal, who seems to have begun writing his Satires about the time that Martial died. The chief difference is in tone and attitude. Juvenal is usually (though not always) in a state of violent indignation (to use his own phrase) at everything he sees – or at least he pretends to be – whereas Martial, for all his dislike of pretension and hypocrisy, generally takes things more calmly.

6
Martial and Patronage

Mention has been made in the first chapter of gifts, in money or in kind, made to Martial by richer friends. It was also explained that a literary career could not bring in a regular income. The question arises of the extent to which he lived the life of a 'client'. To understand this it is necessary to consider the subject of patronage, as experienced in the Roman world.

The idea that a writer might see himself as dependent on the generosity of private individuals is foreign, and rather distasteful, to us today, though dependence on fellowships or grants from charitable foundations is quite acceptable. For example, Christ Church, Oxford, provided a home for W.H. Auden in his latter days, and we are familiar with the concept of the 'artist in residence'.

Matters were different in former times. Dr Johnson's famous definition of 'patron' in his *Dictionary* – 'One who countenances, supports or protects. Commonly a wretch who supports with insolence, and is paid with flattery' – and his lines in *The Vanity of Human Wishes* (159-60) –

There mark what ills the scholar's life assail,
Toil, envy, want, the patron, and the jail

– were inspired by his shoddy treatment by the Earl of Chesterfield.

Johnson's reference to the patron being 'paid with flattery' very much applies to Martial, who makes it quite clear that he expects material rewards in return. Occasionally he jokingly suggests that failure to provide such rewards is a form of cheating. To us this may seem tasteless, but our understanding of the situation in Martial's time is complicated by the fact that there was a system of 'patronage' in existence which did not merely involve literary men, but was a recognised feature of society in general. It was based on a concept of *amicitia* (friendship), which was different from ours in that it involved a system of reciprocity, in the form of goods (presents or loans of money, or gifts in kind) or services (whether political, or legal, or purely social). Interesting evidence of how this might work is provided by Martial 4.40, addressed to a (fictitious) Postumus, whose friendship had meant so much to him, over thirty years, that he preferred him to Piso and the Senecas (noted above as models of generosity). Postumus is now a man of power and wealth, but does nothing for Martial, who says it is too late for him to seek another *rex* (king), and complains to Fortuna, whose reply is that Postumus has cheated her. We see here how friends of equal status have a balanced oblig-

6. Martial and Patronage

ation of reciprocity to each other, whereas inequality obliges the better-off to help the needier. The less well-off may, all the same, be expected to give presents, at the Saturnalia, or on birthdays – described by Martial at 5.48 as 'hooks' to catch fish. He ends that poem with a paradox of the kind he delighted in, arguing that a poor man is generous to a rich friend when he gives him nothing. The dependents and supporters of a rich and powerful man would be dignified with the name *amici*, the essential concept of 'friendship' still being considered important, but the paradoxical nature of the relationship is shown by the fact that it was normal for them to address him as *dominus* – 'master' – as if they were his slaves, and even to refer to him (as above) as their *rex* – a term which had for the Romans, ever since the time of Tarquinius Superbus, a deeply pejorative flavour. Martial even describes himself, in his role as client, as a slave (2.18).

In this context, it is necessary to recall the original meaning of the word *patronus*. It is related to *pater*, and meant something like 'substitute father'. A slave was regarded as not having, in the legal sense, a father, and so when he was freed his former master took on that role, and was called his *patronus*; he was expected to provide him with various kinds of protection. One of these would have been the duty to defend his interests if challenged in a court of law: hence the use of the word *patronus* to mean an advocate. The use of the word for a more powerful man extending similar protection to a less powerful free-born citizen developed from this. The word for the dependent man was *cliens*.

Interesting light is thrown on the nature of the relationship in Horace's time by his story at Epistles 1.7 (published in about 20 BC) of Philippus, a distinguished elderly lawyer, and the auctioneer Vulteius Mena. Philippus happens to spot Mena, and likes the look of him. He sends his slave to ask who he is – *quo sit patre quove patrono* ('who is his father or patron', i.e. whether he is freeborn or a freedman). He is pleased by what he hears, and asks him to dinner. Mena is startled and refuses, but when Philippus next sees him he greets Mena first. Mena's gaffe in failing this social test, and also in not having called on Philippus in the morning, gives Philippus the opportunity to say that he will forgive him if he comes to dinner. Mena does so, and, 'like a fish chasing a hidden hook', becomes *mane cliens, et iam certus conviva* (a client who calls in the morning, and a regular dinner-guest). Philippus takes him out to the country, and is so amused by Mena's ecstatic reaction that he helps to set him up as a farmer. This ends in disaster, and the angry Mena storms back to Philippus, whom he addresses as *patrone*, asking to be restored to his former life. The moral is that gifts ought to be suited to the recipient.

The peculiar, and in many ways mysterious, custom of the *salutatio* (greeting), referred to here by Horace, complicates the whole business even further. It required the 'client' to call on his patron first thing in the morning,

6. Martial and Patronage

wearing his toga, a hot and uncomfortable garment only worn when necessary. He would greet him, and the patron (possibly having to be prompted by his *nomenclator*, a slave employed to remember people's names) would respond. The traditional arrangement was that, if the patron were involved in either political or legal business that day, he might want his clients to accompany him, since a large entourage was a sign of power, and could act as a claque. The clients might, at the end of the day, accompany him to the baths. There they would usually be rewarded with money. It is not clear why the practice described by Juvenal differed, in that he represents the dole as given out at the s*alutatio*, though the simplest explanation is that over the course of years habits had changed (Juvenal's first Satire was probably written some years after Martial's last book).

The word for this 'dole', *sportula*, literally means a small basket, and it is assumed that the original dinner offered to the client (as by Philippus) was replaced with a basket of food, and this in turn by a sum of money. (It is interesting that in two epigrams – 7.86 and 9.85 – Martial uses the word *sportula* to refer to a meal.) By Martial's time the dole was standardised as 100 *quadrantes*. This was a pretty measly sum, though at 3.30 the client needs it to pay for his toga, his rent, his bath, and his prostitute. Elsewhere Martial claims that only 'three or four' can support themselves by means of the *salutatio*. Patrons could, of course, be more generous if they wanted, and Martial refers to some cases (8.42; 9.100; 10.27). If the client was lucky, the patron would invite him to dinner, though here he might be unlucky enough to be entertained with a poorer meal than his host – another situation mentioned by Martial (already referred to in the previous chapter). It later formed the subject of Juvenal's fifth Satire, where the client is just there to be made a fool of, and Juvenal says he deserves what he gets. There was an apparently brief period when an edict of Domitian required patrons to give their clients a *recta cena* (proper dinner) instead of the dole: Martial makes it clear that the loss of the money could make this a doubtful blessing.

The relationship must have had a different dimension when the 'client' was a literary man, since he was in a position to reward his patron's generosity by praising him in his published work. In the case of Martial, Pliny's gift of money for his journey back to Spain, explicitly stated to be in return for the epigram in which Martial praised him, has been mentioned above. The tradition of literary patronage went back a long way: for example, the great early Roman poet Ennius was supported by several leading senators, and Cicero reports a story that his statue was set up in the tomb of the Scipios, the distinguished military commanders and statesmen. Much the most famous literary patron was Augustus' friend and adviser Maecenas, who supported Virgil, Horace, Propertius and other poets. Martial wishes that he could find a similar patron, joking that, if he did, he would be another Virgil (see Chapter 1).

All of the above seems reasonably straightforward, until

6. Martial and Patronage

one starts to ask questions. How many clients did each patron have? And how many patrons did each client have? Did he call on the same patron every day, or on a series of patrons? How often did a patron expect a client to call? How often did a patron expect a client to accompany him all day? These questions are not easy to answer. Martial several times represents patrons as expecting him to call. Sometimes the patron himself is absent – perhaps off to greet a greater man than himself. He even records a consul making his greeting at 'a thousand doorways' (10.10). Martial complains about his loss of time and energy in paying the call – let alone going round all day. At 1.70 he sends his book to present his greetings for him, telling it how to find the way, and assuring it that Proculus' house welcomes poets; it must explain that its master could not write such poems if he made morning calls. He complains about the expense of keeping his toga in good enough shape for the purpose. What is especially remarkable is that in one poem he represents himself as the patron, giving out only the basic 100 *quadrantes*, but aware that his client is likely to have preferred to call on rich men who offer larger sums (8.42). On the other hand 1.80 jokes about a man who died of disappointment because he only received one dole. He must have expected more than one, but it is not easy to see how he would have qualified. And at 10.70 Martial complains that no one pays court to him.

He regularly uses the word *amicus* in describing the relationship, often in the context of behaviour which does not suit the notion of friendship. On the other hand, when complaining that a patron is out greeting another man, he complains that a *rex* ought not to have a *rex*, showing that he does not see it as some kind of social pyramid (2.18). Once Martial suggests the ingenious dodge of sending his own freedman as a substitute, arguing that he can be much more useful in carrying, pushing, and applauding; he says he will provide whatever a freedman cannot (3.46).

It would appear that the combination of *salutatio* and *sportula* probably played comparatively little part in Martial's life, and that the frequent references to the practice are explained by its importance to many less well-connected people (to say nothing of better-connected people), and by its fertility as a theme.

7
Martial and Posterity

As a 'minor' author, and one whose works were for various reasons at different times regarded as offensive, Martial's reputation has reflected the times to a remarkable degree. The earliest author to be substantially influenced by him was his friend Juvenal; the influence is pervasive, but not often easy to pin down. It was regarded as a sign of the trivial taste of Aelius, who was adopted by Hadrian as his successor (but died before him), that he called Martial 'his Virgil'. In late antiquity he was imitated by the poets Ausonius and Luxorius, and quoted by Sidonius Apollinaris. His works survived through the 'Dark Ages'. He was particularly well known in the early Middle Ages in Britain. Godfrey, Prior of the Benedictine abbey of Winchester (*c.* 1050-1107), wrote epigrams after his model, as did Henry of Huntingdon. Giraldus Cambrensis (1146-1223), Archdeacon of Brecon, author of the celebrated *Itinerarium Kambriae*, wrote a number of epigrams, including the lines set over his stall:

>Vive Deo, tibi mors requies, tibi vita labori;
>   vive Deo, mors est vivere, vita mori.

Martial

Live for God; death is rest for you, but life is labour.
Live for God; death is living, life is dying.

Martial's earliest commentator seems to have been an Englishman, John Marre (died 1408), Prior of the Carmelite friary at Doncaster, but his commentary is lost.

Some of the early humanists of North Italy knew him, but it is with Petrarch himself that we first find him influencing the main stream of Italian humanism. Boccaccio possessed an annotated manuscript of Martial, which he may have stolen from Monte Cassino. Much use was made of Martial by the Sicilian poet Antonio Beccadelli, known as 'il Panormita', especially for his notorious *Hermaphroditus*, written *c.* 1425. The humanist Lorenzo Valla, referring to a man who has stolen some of his writings, uses the phrase *plagiaria lex*. The Latin word *plagium* denotes the stealing of someone else's slave, or the forcing of a free man into slavery, and Martial is the only ancient author to use the word of literary theft (at 1.52.9). So it was Martial who was responsible for our modern use of the word 'plagiarism'.

He was one of the first authors whose works were printed. The edition printed at Rome *c.* 1470-71 by Sweynheym and Pannartz was probably the earliest. The first commentary printed (in 1474) was written by a protégé of Poggio Bracciolini, Domizio Calderini (he had already sent a manuscript copy to Lorenzo de' Medici the previous year); it is still useful.

Martial's work was not, however, thought suitable for

7. Martial and Posterity

teaching. Enea Silvio Piccolomini (later Pope Pius II) described him in his treatise on education as *pernitiosus* (pernicious). This moral disapprobation was to grow. The Venetian Andrea Navagero (1483-1529) used to burn volumes of Martial as an offering to Vulcan every year on a day dedicated to the Muses. The great Neapolitan humanist Giovanni Gioviano Pontano, while praising him for his workmanship, human insight, and wit, criticised him not only for his obscenity, but for the biting and sarcastic character of his humour, regarded by Pontano as a Spanish characteristic (see Book III of his *De Sermone*, published in 1519). The matter was charmingly expressed by Timothy Kendal in his *Flowers of Epigrammes* (1577):

> Martial is much mislikt, and lothde,
>   Of modest mynded men,
> For leude, lascivious, wanton woorks
>   And woords whiche he doeth pen.

In 1568 the first bowdlerised edition was published at Antwerp, the work of two French Jesuits, and an Austrian Jesuit, Matthaeus Raderus, produced another in 1599. This provoked an epigram by John Donne:

> Why this man gelded Martiall I muse
> Except himselfe alone his tricks would use,
> As Katherine, for the Courts sake, put downe Stewes.

The point of the bowdlerisation was, of course, to make it possible to use Martial in the classroom, as also in the case of the 'Delphin' edition of 1680 by Vincent Collesson, already referred to. Another celebrated anthology for school use was the *Epigrammatum Delectus*, of which half the contents were by Martial. The editor was Claude Lancelot, professor of theology at Port Royal. It was published in 1659, and was used as a textbook at Eton College throughout much of the eighteenth century.

In the sixteenth and seventeenth centuries annotated editions were published in the Netherlands, putting the interpretation of Martial onto a new level. There was also an edition by the English schoolmaster Thomas Farnaby (1605). This was the period when Martial's work was at its most influential, especially on the many authors of Latin verse. Conspicuous examples are Erasmus (who also often quotes Martial in his *Adagia*), and his friend Thomas More, whose epigrams (published at Basel in 1518) were enormously popular and influential on other authors. Another Briton known throughout Europe was the Caernarfonshire-born schoolmaster John Owen (*c.* 1564-1628), known as Johannes Audoenus, Cambro-Britannicus. Said to have been the best-selling poems of the seventeenth century, his Latin epigrams were translated into English, German, French, Spanish and Danish. It is claimed that they show the influence of Welsh poetical techniques in rhyming and musical effects.

7. Martial and Posterity

One of the first English translations of Martial is by Henry Howard, Earl of Surrey (*c*. 1517-47), first printed among his 'Songes and Sonettes' in *Tottel's Miscellany* (1557). It is a version of 10.47 (see p. 21), which is addressed – like 5.20 (p. 19) – to Martial's friend Julius Martialis.

> Martiall, the thinges that do attayne
> The happy life, be these, I finde.
> The richesse left, not got with pain:
> The frutefull ground: the quiet mynde:
> The egall frend, no grudge, no strife:
> No charge of rule, nor governance:
> Without disease the healthfull lyfe:
> The houshold of continuance:
> The meane diet, no delicate fare:
> Trew wisdom ioyned with simplenesse:
> The night discharged of all care,
> Where wine the wit may not oppresse:
> The faithful wife, without debate:
> Suche slepes, as may begyle the night:
> Contented with thine owne estate,
> Ne wish for death, ne feare his might.

It is given particular poignancy by Howard's life of strife and soldiery, and his unjust execution at the age of thirty. Howard's is one of an astonishing number of translations of this epigram made in sixteenth-century Britain.

Vernacular authors in England are deeply indebted to

Martial

Martial, including Sir John Harington, Ben Jonson, and Robert Herrick. Shakespeare knew him, and it has recently been suggested by M.R. Clark that he refers to him in *Twelfth Night*, when Sir Toby Belch is telling Sir Andrew Aguecheek how to write a challenge to a duel:

'Go, write it in a martial hand, be curst and brief. It is no matter how witty so it be eloquent and full of invention ... Let there be gall enough in thy ink' (3.2.39f.).

In *The New Oxford Book of Seventeenth-Century Verse* (1991), Alastair Fowler writes; 'No recovered genre was more significant historically than epigram ... Indeed, the most important literary change of the century could be seen as the pervasive tendency whereby epigram merged with and transformed almost every other kind.'

In France Martial's earliest and most enthusiastic imitator was Clément Marot (*Deux livres d'épigrammes*, 1538), and other poets who owed much to him include Du Bellay, Ronsard and Baïf. Montaigne and Boileau make use of his work. Spanish writers naturally felt a special affinity with their compatriot. Many German poets of the seventeenth century wrote translations, but a real oddity was the bizarre Christianised version by Johannes Burmeister (*Martialis Renati Parodiae Sacrae*, 1612). The Anglican divine Jeremy Taylor often quotes Martial.

One of the most famous of all adaptations of Martial dates from the late seventeenth century, but its origin is far from clear. The poem in question is 1.32:

7. Martial and Posterity

> Non amo te, Sabidi, nec possum dicere quare:
> hoc tantum possum dicere, non amo te.

> I don't like you, Sabidius, but I can't say why: I can only say that I don't like you.

The story goes that Tom Brown (described in Henry Fielding's *Tom Jones* as 'one of the greatest wits that ever the nation produced'), when up at Oxford, was threatened by Dr Fell, the Dean of Christ Church, with being sent down, but was offered forgiveness on condition that he translate Martial's epigram extempore, which he did:

> I do not love you Dr Fell, but why I cannot tell;
> But this I know full well, I do not love you, Dr Fell.

The story cannot be true, but the irony is that Dr Fell, despite his distinction in other ways, is chiefly known because of it, and it has unfairly affected his reputation.

The poem was discussed at length by the Earl of Chesterfield, who referred to a man he much admired, but could not love. Boswell and others thought that this was Dr Johnson, but Johnson maintained that it referred to George Lyttelton. Chesterfield's opinion of Martial was not high; he wrote to his son, 'Martial has wit, and is worth your looking into sometimes; but I recommend the Greek epigrams to your supreme contempt.' He did, however, refer to 'Horace, Virgil, Terence, and Martial, who are the most famous Latin poets', and himself produced a neat epigram, defining the epigram (in fact, a version of an anonymous Latin couplet):

> The qualities rare in a bee that we meet,
>   In an epigram never should fail;
> The body should always be little and sweet
>   And a sting should be left in its tail.

Dr Johnson's bluestocking friend, Mrs Thrale (of Streatham), made a collection of translations of 1.13 (the epigram on Arria's suicide) over many years. Comparison of Martial with the Greeks was a popular topic; Montesquieu preferred Martial, Voltaire the Greeks.

The appreciation of wit in the eighteenth century meant that Martial was highly valued. A charming instance is provided by Sir Thomas Parkyns (1662-1741), the 'Wrestling Baronet', of Bunny, Nottinghamshire, who could 'throw a tenant, combat a paradox, quote Martial, or sign a mittimus with any man of his age or country' (*Retrospective Review*, 11.161). Some of the epigrams which appealed then seem less attractive to us. An example is 1.19 (already much imitated in the sixteenth and seventeenth centuries, for example by Sir John Harington, Marot, Crashaw, and Herrick):

> Si memini, fuerant tibi quattuor, Aelia, dentes:
>   expulit una duos tussis et una duos.

7. Martial and Posterity

    iam secura potes totis tussire diebus:
        nil istic quod agat tertia tussis habet.

If I remember rightly, you had four teeth, Aelia. One cough knocked out two, and another knocked out two more. Now you can cough all day without worrying; there's nothing left for a third to do.

Aelia is presumably old: the common theme of the attack on an old woman has been mentioned above (p. 74). In one of Joseph Addison's contributions to the *Tatler*, in 1710, a letter from 'Pasquin of Rome' relates that 'there has lately been found a human tooth in a catacomb, which has engaged a couple of convents in a lawsuit; each of them pretending that it belonged to the jawbone of a saint who was of their order'. A speech has been made by a cardinal, 'who, by reason of its being found out of the company of any other bones, asserted that it might be one of the teeth which was coughed out by Aelia, an old woman whose loss is recorded by Martial'.

A notorious translation into English was made by the Scotsman James Elphinston (who kept a 'Jacobite seminary' in Kensington). It was published in 1782, with a grand list of subscribers. The poems were rearranged by subject, and in his pompous and contorted preface Elphinston boasts: 'From all will so conjunctly and so severally beam that piety, morality, and love of order which unvitiated Nature has rendered inseparable from Sensibility and Reason' ... 'Here, the first time in seventeen centuries, have his works been illuminated by arrangement.' Two short examples will give the flavour of his translations. First, his version of 1.32 (for Tom Brown's, see above): 'Sabby, I love thee not, nor can say why. One thing I can say, Sab: thee love not I'. And secondly, that of 2.42: 'Why in the tub thy parts posterior lay? Thy head, immerg'd, would it and thee bewray'. The epigrams were followed by a hundred pages of 'Comment'. The book was savagely attacked by Robert Burns. Asked what he thought of it, he wrote on a blank leaf:

> O thou, whom Poesy abhors,
> Whom Prose has turned out of doors!
> Heard'st thou that groan? Proceed no further:
> 'Twas laurelled Martial roaring 'Murther'!

The early Romantics, including Goethe and Coleridge, read and imitated Martial. The dramatist G.E. Lessing, already referred to in Chapter 2 for his contribution to the theory of the epigram, and notable also for his contribution to the interpretation of Martial, produced several imitations. The Italian tragic poet Vittorio Alfieri wrote numerous epigrams between 1783 and 1798. This is an example:

> L'uom che in un sol sonetto
>   Ha un po' di me mal detto,
>   Io credero che amico ognor mi sia
>   Fin ch'ei scrive tragedie in lode mia.

7. Martial and Posterity

The man who in just one sonnet has abused me a bit,
I shall believe that he is still my friend, until he writes
tragedies in my praise.

A milder author of epigrams was Filippo Pananti, whose works were published in Florence in 1824. Here is one:

Un astronomo inglese
    Dei viaggi di Cook fece il rapporto.
    Quanti ne ha fatti? una contessa chiese:
    Tre, rispose; e la dama: in quale è morto?

An English astronomer recounted the journeys of Cook. How many did he make? asked a countess. Three, he replied; and the lady: on which did he die?

The nineteenth century, however, saw a steep decline in Martial's reputation. His type of wit was generally despised, and his impropriety seemed inexcusable. Hence the attitude of Donna Inez, who, in arranging the education of her son Don Juan, 'most desired ... that his breeding should be strictly moral' (Lord Byron, *Don Juan*, I.39). As Byron puts it (I.43-5):

'I can't help thinking Juvenal was wrong,
    Although no doubt his real intent was good,
For speaking out so plainly in his song,
    So much indeed as to be downright rude;

Martial

And then what proper person can be partial
To all those nauseous epigrams of Martial?

Juan was taught from out the best edition,
    Expurgated by learned men, who place,
Judiciously, from out the schoolboy's vision
    The grosser parts; but fearful to deface
Too much their modest bard by this omission,
    And pitying sore his mutilated case,
They only add them all in an appendix,
Which saves in fact the trouble of an index;

For there we have them all at one fell swoop,
    Instead of being scatter'd through the pages;
They stand forth marshall'd in a handsome troop,
    To meet the ingenuous youth of future ages,
Till some less rigid editor shall stoop
    To call them back into their separate cages,
Instead of standing staring altogether
Like garden gods – and not so decent either.

The 'best edition' was that of Collesson, mentioned above. Byron's words have sometimes been taken as his own opinion – absurdly, for his recent editor Jerome J. McGann describes them as 'an ironic defence of *Don Juan*, attacked for supposed indecency'. Martial was actually one of Byron's favourite authors, and he made translations or imitations of a number of his poems. Here is his version of 6.53:

7. Martial and Posterity

Jack supped – and drank – and went to bed,
Morn breaks – and finds the sleeper dead.
What caused this healthy man's perdition?
Alas! He dreamt of his Physician.

And here is his 'comment' on 10.46, in *Don Juan* (15.21):

'Omnia vult belle Matho dicere – dic aliquando
    Et bene, dic neutrum, dic aliquando male.'
The first is rather more than mortal can do;
    The second may be sadly done or gaily;
The third is still more difficult to stand to;
    The fourth we hear, and see, and say too, daily:
The whole together is what I could wish
To serve in this conundrum of a dish.

Despite moral disapproval, the epigrams could all the same be useful fodder for schools – just the fate Martial hoped to avoid (1.35 and 8.3) – in the form of 'Selections'. It could be argued that this was justified by Martial's own suggestions that readers might pick and choose (10.1; 13.3.8; see also p. 54), but, as already pointed out, that is ironic self-denigration. It was inevitable that, so long as he was only known in this travestied form, he was regarded as trivial and not worth taking seriously.

Nevertheless, the Scottish schoolmaster Dr Craufurd Tait Ramage, although he considered Martial 'a base flatterer, and ... a most indecent writer', included no less than fourteen pages of passages from Martial in his popular anthology *Beautiful Thoughts from Latin Authors* (London, 1864).

Occasionally a poet of calibre, such as A.C. Swinburne or José-Maria de Heredia, produced the odd imitation, but these were exceptional. One poet who thought for himself was Robert Louis Stevenson. He wrote: 'in this age, when we all lean to the reading of light verses, Martial, the neatest of versifiers, the wittiest of men, is passed over with contempt; and either no one reads, or everyone considers it decent to dissemble having read him'. In 1887 he wrote that we 'find in this unseemly jester's serious passages the image of a kind, wise and self-respecting gentleman', while the neglect of such passages 'is one among a thousand things that help to build up our distorted and hysterical conception of the great Roman Empire'. He told John Addington Symonds, 'I cannot conceive a person who does not love his Martial.' Stevenson's *Collected Poems* include sixteen translations, including this one of 10.23:

> Now Antonius, in a smiling age,
> Counts of his life the fifteenth finished stage*.
> The rounded days and the safe years he sees
> Nor fears death's water mounting round his knees.
> To him remembering not one day is sad,
> Not one but that its memory makes him glad.

* 15 Olympiads, i.e. 75 years

7. Martial and Posterity

So good men lengthen life; and to recall
The past, is to have twice enjoyed it all.

A contemporary of Stevenson who also knew his Martial was Herman Melville, who quotes 4.5.1-2 in chapter 2 of *Billy Budd, Foretopman* (completed in 1891), as

> the good-natured poet's famous invocation, near two thousand years ago, of the good rustic out of his latitude in the Rome of the Caesars:
>
> Honest and poor, faithful in word and thought,
>   What has thee, Fabian, to the city brought?'

It was at this time that the full weight of German scholarship was brought to bear on Martial, with serious study of the text (in fact transmitted to us in a healthy state, when compared with those of other authors), and the hefty commentary by the polymath Ludwig Friedlaender (1886), whose work as a historian of Roman society explains his interest in Martial.

The obscenity which put so many people off Martial was just what attracted others to him. Beccadelli has been mentioned above. An early nineteenth-century edition whose title page refers to it as a 'Nouvelle Traduction', and gives the place of publication as 'À Paphos, de l'Imprimerie du Dieu des Amours', must have sadly frustrated those in search of spice, as it simply omits the less proper poems. More enterprising was Giuspanio Graglia, of Turin, who published in London in 1782 a complete translation, and whose versions of the obscene poems were printed by H.G. Bohn in his 'Bohn's Classical Library' edition of 1859, and again by W.C.A. Ker in his 'Loeb Classical Library' edition of 1925. Bohn praised Graglia as 'rather dexterous in refining impurities'.

Quite the opposite line is taken in a curious book called *Index Expurgatorius of Martial, Literally Translated, Comprising all the Epigrams hitherto omitted by English translators*, privately printed and published anonymously in 1868. The authors have been identified as Captain Edward Sellon (an author of erotic novels, who had committed suicide in 1866), George Augustus Sala (a well-known journalist and bohemian who shared his friend Swinburne's taste for flagellation), and two other 'Oxford men'. The prose and verse translations sometimes manage to be more obscene than the originals, and the lengthy notes are full of strange and recondite information. It will have been a version such as this which helped to stimulate the 'filthy thoughts' of the hero of E.M. Forster's *Maurice* (written in 1913-14): 'the school library was immaculate, but while at his grandfather's he came across an unexpurgated Martial, and stumbled about in it with burning ears'. Some of the more recent versions, such as those of Brian Hill (*Ganymede in Rome* [1971], and *An Eye for Ganymede* [1972]) make their intended audience clear by the selection of poems and coyly pederastic frontispieces. More

7. Martial and Posterity

recently still Thierry Martin's French translations have been published (2000) by 'Gaykitsch Camp'.

One scholar for whom Martial's obscenity was no deterrent was A.E. Housman, who devoted numerous articles to the discussion of problems in his text and interpretation. Nevertheless, his discussion of various sexual matters, published in *Hermes* in 1931 with the title 'Praefanda', was written in Latin, through editorial deference to the sensibilities of the day.

Today's sexual frankness, not to say exhibitionism, has made anxieties about 'obscenity' seem very old-fashioned. The new Loeb Classical Library edition, by D.R. Shackleton Bailey (1993) makes no bones about translating everything. This is much the most accessible and reliable edition – Shackleton Bailey having also published the best modern text of Martial, in 1990.

The undervaluation, if not contempt, which affected Martial's reputation for almost a century after Friedlaender's edition has, over the last thirty years, been reversed, and almost every book now has a modern commentary (sometimes more than one), in English, Italian, or German. There are good general studies by J.P. Sullivan and (in German) by Niklas Holzberg, and a number of monographs on individual topics. Happily it can be said that Martial's time has come again.

The revival of interest over the last forty years has led a number of poets to translate his work into English. In 1973 James Michie, who had already translated Catullus and the Odes of Horace, published a substantial selection, republished with corrections in 1978 in the Penguin Classics series. Two poets who published smaller collections were Peter Porter (*After Martial*, 1972) and Tony Harrison (*U.S. Martial*, 1981 – written in New York). In 1987 J.P. Sullivan and Peter Whigham edited *Epigrams of Martial Englished by Divers Hands*, a bulky compilation of versions dating from between the sixteenth century and contemporary times, the largest number being by Whigham himself. In 1996 another collection, under the title *Martial in English*, appeared in the Penguin Classics series; again J.P. Sullivan was the editor, but after his death in 1993 the task was completed by A.J. Boyle. In this case the contents were arranged chronologically. Despite the title, they include poems more or less in the manner of Martial as well as actual translations.

Further Reading

Much the most convenient and up-to-date edition of Martial is the three-volume set in the Loeb Classical Library (Harvard University Press, 1993) by D.R. Shackleton Bailey. This has the Latin on one page, with English translation opposite, brief notes, an index of topics, and a particularly useful index of names. There are also commentaries in English, including prose translations, of the *Liber Spectaculorum*, by Kathleen Coleman (Oxford University Press, 2006), of Book I, by Peter Howell (Athlone Press, London, 1980), of Book II, by Craig Williams (Oxford University Press, 2004), of Book IV, by Rosario Moreno Soldevila (Brill, Leiden, 2006), of Book V, by Peter Howell (Aris and Phillips, Warminster, 1995), of Book VII, by Guillermo Galan Vioque (Brill, Leiden, 2002), of Book XI, by Nigel Kay (Duckworth, London, 1985), and of Book XIII (the *Xenia*) (Duckworth, 2001), and Book XIV (the *Apophoreta*) (Duckworth, 1996), both by T.J. Leary. The commentary on Book IX by Christer Henriksén (Acta Universitatis Upsaliensis, Uppsala, 1998-9) is in English, but does not include translations. All of these contain bibliographies, but for the fullest account of recent publications there are two articles in *Lustrum* by Sven Lorenz (45, 2003, 167-277; 48, 2006, 109-223).

Martial – Select Epigrams, edited by Lindsay and Patricia Watson (Cambridge University Press, 2003) provides translations and helpful commentaries.

J.P. Sullivan's *Martial: The Unexpected Classic – A Literary and Historical Study* (Cambridge University Press, 1991) is the essential monograph, though it presents a somewhat unsympathetic portrait of its subject, taxing him with misogyny and other forms of 'political incorrectness', and underplaying his humour.

Most of the essays in *Toto Notus in Orbe: Perspektiven der Martial-Interpretation*, edited by Farouk Grewing (Franz Steiner Verlag, Stuttgart, 1998), are in English. Martial's relationship with his predecessors is the subject of B.W. Swann's *Martial's Catullus* (Hildesheim, 1994), and Gideon Nisbet's *Greek Epigram in the Roman Empire: Martial's Forgotten Rivals* (Oxford University Press, 2003).

William Fitzgerald has provided a modern literary study in *Martial: The World of the Epigram* (University of Chicago Press, 2007). There are also significant articles by Luke Roman, on 'The Representation of Literary Materiality in Martial's Epigrams' (*Journal of Roman Studies* 91, 2001,113-45), and by Stephen Hinds, on 'Martial's Ovid / Ovid's Martial' (*Journal of Roman Studies* 97, 2007, 113-54). Martial's role as a critic of contemporary society is discussed by Art L. Spisak in *Martial: A Social Guide* (Duckworth, 2007).

Further Reading

The revised dating of the *Liber Spectaculorum* has been argued by T.V. Buttrey in 'Domitian, the Rhinoceros, and the Date of Martial's *Liber de Spectaculis*', in *Journal of Roman Studies* 97, 2007, 101-12.

J.N. Adams, in *The Latin Sexual Vocabulary* (Duckworth, 1982), has much to say about Martial.

The vexed question of the publication of Martial's poems, whether initially in collections of a few epigrams circulated informally, or in *codices* (parchment books) containing several books at once, has been discussed by Peter White in 'The Presentation and Dedication of the *Silvae* and the *Epigrams*' (*Journal of Roman Studies* 64, 1974, 40-61), challenged by Don Fowler in 'Martial and the Book' (*Ramus* 24, 1995, 31-58), to whom White replied in 'Martial and Pre-publication Texts' (*Échos du Monde Classique / Classical Views* 40, 1996, 397-412).

The best account of Roman social life is J.P.V.D. Balsdon's *Life and Leisure in Ancient Rome* (Bodley Head, London, 1969). The well-known book by Jérome Carcopino, *Daily Life in Ancient Rome* (translated by E.O. Lorimer, Penguin, Harmondsworth, 1941) needs to be used with caution. There is also Ugo Enrico Paoli, *Rome: Its People, Life and Customs* (translated by R.D. Mcnaghten, Longman, London, 1963). A more positive view of Domitian than the traditional one is presented in Brian W. Jones's *The Emperor Domitian* (Routledge, London, 1992).

On Callimachus, see Alan Cameron, *Callimachus and his Critics* (Princeton University Press, 1995). See also his

The Greek Anthology from Meleager to Planudes (Clarendon Press, 1993), together with *Brill's Companion to Hellenistic Epigram*, edited by Peter Bing and Jon Steffen Bruss (Brill, Leiden, 2007). The newly discovered fragments of Posidippus are discussed in a book edited by Kathryn Gutzwiller, *The New Posidippus: A Hellenistic Poetry Book* (Oxford University Press, 2005).

An interesting critical essay by a non-classicist is H.A. Mason's 'Is Martial a Classic?' (*Cambridge Quarterly* 17, 1988, 297-368), a review of Sullivan and Whigham's anthology of translations mentioned in the last chapter. M.R. Clark's *'In a Martial hand': Studies in the Epigram in Early Modern Britain* (D.Phil. thesis, Oxford, 2002) has not yet been published: it deals with Thomas More, John Parkhurst, John Owen, Thomas Campion, Ben Jonson, Robert Herrick, and William Shakespeare.

Index

Adams, J.N., 51-2
Addison, J., 109
Aelius, 101
Agricola, 66
Alexis, 13-14
Alfieri, V., 110
Anne, Queen, 70
Anthologia Latina, 55
Antipater of Sidon, 44
Antony, 43
Apicius, 83
Aquileia, 23
arches, 69
Archilochus, 36
Asinius Pollio, 14
Auden, W.H., 93
Augustus, 10, 16, 43, 69, 98
Ausonius, 101

Baiae, 79
Baïf, J.A. de, 106
Bailey, D.R.S., 117
Balanchine, G., 89
Balsdon, J.P.V.D., 80
Barnum and Bailey, 89
baths, 79-82, 97
Beccadelli, A., 102, 115
Bilbilis, 9-10, 23-4, 26, 29-30
Boccaccio, G., 102

Bohn, H.G., 116
Boileau, N., 106
Boswell, J., 107
Boyle, A.J., 118
Britain, 59
Brown, Tom, 107, 110
Brutus, 43
Burmeister, J., 106
Burns, Robert, 110
Buttrey, T.V., 15
Byron, Lord, 51, 54, 111-13

Calatayud, 9-10
Calderini, D., 102
Callimachus, 14, 36, 39, 41, 44
Calvus, 41
Cambridge History of Latin Literature, 60
Catalepton, 44
Cato the Elder, 64, 75
Cato the Younger, 15, 28, 50-1
Catullus, 26, 41-5, 50-1, 117
censorship, 64-5
Chesterfield, Earl of, 94, 107-8
Christ Church, Oxford, 93, 107

Index

Cicero, 28, 43
Cinna, 55-6
Circus, 90
Clark, M.R., 106
Claudius (emperor), 12, 83
Claudius Etruscus, 79
Coleridge, S.T., 35, 46, 110
Collesson, V., 51, 104, 112
Colosseum, 15
Columella, 11
Constantinus Cephalas, 37
Crashaw, R., 108
cycles, 53
Cyrillus, 44

Demodocus, 36
dinner-parties, 21, 38, 66, 82-4, 98
Domitian, 11, 15-16, 18, 26, 54, 63-71, 89-90, 98
Donne, John, 103
Du Bellay, J., 106

Elizabeth, Queen, 70
Elphinstone, J., 109
Ennius, 40, 42-3, 98
epic, 14-15
equites, 16, 63-4
Erasmus, 104
Erotion, 77-8
Eton, 104

Farnaby, T., 104
Fell, Dr, 107
flattery, 26, 63-71, 93-4
Forster, E.M., 116
Fortuny Marsal, Marian, 73

Forum Cornelii, 22
Fowler, A., 106
Friedlaender, L., 115, 117
Fronto and Flaccilla, 9
Fulvia, 43

Gaetulicus, 43
Gellius, 41
Getia, 59
Giraldus Cambrensis, 101
Godfrey of Winchester, 101
Goethe, J.W. von, 110
Graglia, G., 116
Greek Anthology, 37, 90, 107

Hadrian, 101
Haile Selassie, 64
Handel, G.F., 84
Harington, Sir J., 106, 108
Harrison, Tony, 118
Henry of Huntingdon, 101
Heredia, J.-M. de, 114
Herrick, R., 106, 108
Highet, G., 29
Hill, Brian, 116
Hispania Tarraconensis, 9
Holzberg, N., 117
Homer, 35
Horace, 40, 53, 61, 74, 90, 96, 98, 107, 117
Housman, A.E., 117
Howard, Henry, 105

Index Expurgatorius of Martial, 116
ius trium liberorum, 15-16, 32

Index

Jalón, River, 9
James I, 64, 71
Johnson, S., 93-4, 107-8
Jonson, B., 71, 78, 84
Julius Caesar, 41, 43
Juvenal, 11-12, 20-1, 29-31, 49, 51, 61, 67-8, 82-3, 90-1, 97-8, 101, 111

Kendal, T., 103
Ker, W.C.A., 116
Klopstock, F.G., 47-8

Lancelot, C., 104
Leary, T.J., 56
Lessing, G.E., 46-7, 110
Licinianus, 23-6
Lucan, 10, 15, 57, 67
Lucilius, 40
Lucillius, 37, 39, 76
Lutatius Catulus, Q., 41
Luxorius, 101
Lyttelton, G., 107

McGann, J.J., 112
Mackail, J.W., 46, 63-4
Maecenas, 14, 98
Mamurra, 43
Marot, C., 106, 108
Marre, J., 102
marriage, 16, 32
Marsus, 43
Martialis, Julius, 19, 21, 32-3, 105
Martin, T., 117
Mayhew, H., 79
Medici, Lorenzo de', 102

Meleager, 37
Melville, H., 115
metre, 35-7, 40, 44-6, 47, 52-4
Michie, J., 117
Moncayo, 10, 24
Montaigne, M.E. de, 106
Montesquieu, C., 108
More, T., 104
Murray, J., 54
Mussolini, B., 64

Navagero, A., 103
Nero, 15, 37, 67, 69, 89
Nerva, 26, 43, 51, 70
Nicarchus, 39
Nomentum, 18, 31

Owen, J., 104

Palatine, 66, 68-9
Pananti, F., 111
Parkyns, Sir T., 108
Parmenion, 44
patronage, 11, 32, 93-100
Pedo, 43
Petrarch, 102
Philip of Thessalonica, 37, 74-5
Piccolomini, E.S., 103
Piso, C. Calpurnius, 11, 16, 66, 94
plagiarism, 21, 102
Pliny the Elder, 84
Pliny the Younger, 20, 27-9, 32, 36, 38, 43, 46, 52, 70, 84, 98

Index

Poggio Bracciolini, G.F., 102
Pompeii, 41, 87
Pompey, 41, 55
Pontano, G.G., 103
Port Royal, 104
Porter, P., 118
Posidippus, 39

Quintilian, 11-12, 50, 67
Quirinal, 18

Rabirius, 69
Raderus, M., 103
Ramage, C.T., 113
Ravenna, 85
recitation, 20-1, 26
rhetoric, 10, 37, 54, 61, 67
Ribota, River, 9
Ronsard, P., 106

Sala, G.A., 116
salutatio, 19-20, 96-9
Sarmatians, 90
Saturnalia, 51, 56, 95
Scipios, 40, 98
Sellar and Yeatman, 68
Sellon, E., 116
Seneca the Younger, 18, 43, 66
Senecas, 11, 66, 94
Shakespeare, W., 106
shows, 15, 63, 68, 87-9
Sidonius Apollinaris, 101
slaves, 18, 31, 38, 77-8, 97
sleep, 29-31, 77
Spain, 9-10, 13, 23-6, 29, 59
Statius, 15, 65-6, 79

Stevenson, R.L., 114
Stoics, 66
Stravinsky, I., 89
Suetonius, 67-9, 87
Sulla, 43
Sullivan, J., 44, 117-18
Sura, 26
Sweynheym and Pannartz, 102
Swinburne, A.C., 114, 116
Symonds, J.A., 114

Tacitus, 66, 68
Tagus, River, 10, 25
Tarquinius Superbus, 95
Tatler, 109
Taylor, J., 106
Terence, 107
Thrale, Mrs, 108
Thrasea, 66
Tiberius, 43, 87
Titus, 15-16, 18, 63
toga, 22, 24-5, 29-30, 97
Trajan, 18, 26, 39, 67, 70

Valerius Maximus, 50
Valla, L., 102
Vienne, 59
Vindelicia, 59
Virgil, 14, 43-4, 55-6, 98, 101, 107
Voltaire, 108

Wernicke, C., 35
Whigham, P., 118
Windsor, 70